FULL MOON RITUAL MASTERY

Lunar Manifesting Secrets & Spirit Clearing Rituals They Don't Want You To Know About (New Moon Astrology & Spiritual Cleansing 2 in 1 Collection)

ANGELA GRACE

© Copyright 2021 - All rights reserved.

The content contained within this book may not be reproduced, duplicated or transmitted without direct written permission from the author or the publisher.

Under no circumstances will any blame or legal responsibility be held against the publisher, or author, for any damages, reparation, or monetary loss due to the information contained within this book, either directly or indirectly.

Legal Notice:

This book is copyright protected. It is only for personal use. You cannot amend, distribute, sell, use, quote or paraphrase any part, or the content within this book, without the consent of the author or publisher.

Disclaimer Notice:

Please note the information contained within this document is for educational and entertainment purposes only. All effort has been executed to present accurate, up to date, reliable, complete information. No warranties of any kind are declared or implied. Readers acknowledge that the author is not engaged in the rendering of legal, financial, medical or professional advice. The content within this book has been derived from various sources. Please consult a licensed professional before attempting any techniques outlined in this book.

By reading this document, the reader agrees that under no circumstances is the author responsible for any losses, direct or indirect, that are incurred as a result of the use of the information contained within this document, including, but not limited to, errors, omissions, or inaccuracies.

CONTENTS

Claim Your *BONUS* Manifesting Toolkit   vii

PART I
New Moon Astrology   1
Lunar Cycle Mastery, How to Say "I Told You So", & Spiritual Energy Meditations

Introduction   3

1. MOON PHASE MASTERY: YOU ARE HOLDING THE KEY TO UNLIMITED POWER   7
   Understanding Moon Phases   8

2. ACTIVATING YOUR POWER INFUSED ONENESS WITH THE MOON   14
   Impact of the Moon on Human Behavior   16

3. WHAT ARE YOU WAITING FOR? HOW TO EASILY TRANSFORM YOUR LIFE WITH MOON PHASES   21
   Flowing With the Dynamics of the Moon   24

4. THE LAW OF ATTRACTION ON STEROIDS: MANIFESTING MASTERY WITH THE MOON PHASES   30
   Wishing on the Moon   32

5. HOW TO DROP JAWS AND SAY "I TOLD YOU SO" WITH LUNAR FUELED SUPER-ABILITIES   42
   Predicting the Different Moon Phases   46

6. WHAT THEY DON'T TELL YOU ABOUT ZODIAC SIGNS   55
   How to Read Your Astrological Chart   56

7. BUILDING THE TOWERING ARCHITECTURE THAT IS YOUR DREAM LIFE: MOON LIFE PLANNING MASTERY	64
A Look at the Daily Moon	66
8. BATHE IN THE MOON'S ENERGY TO CLEANSE WHAT NO LONGER SERVES YOU	73
Healing Yourself With the Energy of the Moon	74
9. THE NEXT LEVEL: MOON MAGIC MASTERY	79
Meditations and Rituals for the Full Moon	80
10. POWER CHARGED MOON CYCLE AND NEW MOON ASTROLOGY GUIDED MEDITATIONS	85
Guided Meditation to Manifest Your Dreams	86
Guided Meditation to Clear Financial Blocks & Attract Money	88
Guided Meditation for Inner Healing	89
Guided Meditation With the Angels to Bring Etheric Energy into Your Life	91
11. THE LUNAR MASTERY 30-MINUTE DAILY RITUAL TO SKYROCKET YOUR EXISTENCE	94
Daily Ritual Formula	95
Afterword	103
References	107
PART II	
Spiritual Cleansing	111
Soul Cleansing Secrets No One Talks About & How To Cleanse Negative Energy From Your House In 7 Days	
Introduction	113
12. CHAPTER 1: YOU, YOUR FAMILY, YOUR PETS, YOUR FOOD, THE TREES OUTSIDE AND EVERYTHING ELSE ARE ALL UNIVERSAL ENERGY	120

13. CHAPTER 2: MEET YOUR ADVERSARIES; THE EVIL EYE, NEGATIVE ENERGY AND DARK FORCES — 127
14. CHAPTER 3: AURA MASTERY, WHAT YOU NEED TO KNOW TO MANIFEST A JOYFUL EXISTENCE — 134
15. CHAPTER 4: SUPERCHARGING YOUR VIBRATION, QUIETING THE MIND, & TOWERING ABOVE NEGATIVE FORCES — 142
16. CHAPTER 5: CASTING YOUR IMPENETRABLE FORCE FIELD OF DEFENSE — 151
17. CHAPTER 6: BEAUTIFY YOUR HOME, BEAUTIFY YOUR EXISTENCE — 163
18. CHAPTER 7: THE WAR YOU ARE DESTINED TO WIN! — 175
19. CHAPTER 8: CLEANSE YOUR OWN ENERGETIC FIELD TO SKYROCKET YOUR JOY — 183
20. CHAPTER 9: WHAT IS WITHIN, WILL BECOME A REALITY ON THE OUTSIDE. MAKE WHAT IS WITHIN BEAUTIFUL — 192
21. CHAPTER 10: AMAZING GUIDED MEDITATIONS TO BANISH NEGATIVE ENTITIES, CLEANSE YOUR AURA AND SUPERCHARGE YOUR LIFE — 200
22. CHAPTER 11: THE 7 DAY NEGATIVE ENERGY CLEANSE RITUAL TO ENCHANT YOUR HOME WITH ANGELIC POWER — 209
23. AFTERWORD — 217

References — 221
Please Leave a Review on Amazon — 225
Join Our Community — 227
Claim Your FREE Audiobook — 229

CLAIM YOUR *BONUS* MANIFESTING TOOLKIT

Are you DONE with settling for a mediocre life, wasting precious time, & ready to live your wildest fantasies?

• Hack your brain, boost performance, & release blocks holding you back from greatness

• Awaken this amazing energy to supercharge your manifestations

• Stop wasting what little precious time you have on ineffective methods

Manifesting Toolkit Includes:

1. **Supercharged Manifestation EFT Tapping Video** Download To Banish Limiting Beliefs & Propel You Toward Your Dream Life (Infused with 432 Hz Frequency)

2. **Secret Formula Journal** Daily manifestation Ritual Done For You. Simply Rinse & Repeat At Home. (You Can Print This Out, Stick On Your Wall, & Cross Off The Days You Complete The Ritual)

3. **Powerful 10 Minute 'Shifting Your reality' Guided Meditation** MP3 Download (Infused with 528 Hz Frequency)

4. ***BONUS*** LOA boosting 10 Minute 'Feminine Energy Awakening' Guided Meditation MP3 Download
Go Here to Get Your *BONUS* Manifesting Toolkit: **bit.ly/manifestingforwomen**

❧ I ☙
NEW MOON ASTROLOGY

Lunar Cycle Mastery, How to Say "I Told You So", & Spiritual Energy Meditations

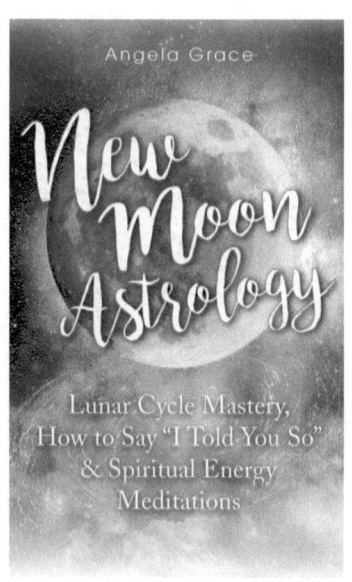

INTRODUCTION

What do you feel when you look at the Moon? Do you just admire its beauty and mystical presence in the sky or do you feel a deeper connection? I am guessing that it is the latter which has brought you here. You are right, as the Moon does hold special powers and comes with a great energetic field that affects all creatures on Earth. It moves eternally in orbit around the Earth and influences the water, nature, animals, and human beings on so many different levels. The whole presence of the Moon is magical, transcendental, and filled with amazing secrets waiting to be unveiled.

Have you been feeling super excited under the full moon? Do you often find yourself drained of all energy when the Moon is not there for you to see? Although you might find it hard to believe, the Moon and other celestial objects can have a dramatic impact on your life. They can affect you emotionally, physically, and mentally. So you can feel depressed without any solid reason or your mood can be lifted in an instant instead. Sometimes you get an energy boost, while at other times within a lunar cycle you feel down and need to rest. So many people miss out on their full potential because they cannot understand what is going on in their life. They feel estranged by nature, out of tune and completely alone.

However, you can totally harness the energy of the Moon and use it to your advantage! You don't need to remain idle and suffer through these energy fluctuations every month, and you should not go through these changes without trying to interpret them. Instead, you can take matters into your own hands and benefit from the mystical power of the Moon. On top of that, you can master the art of astrology and find out how the planets, the houses, and the zodiac signs can work in your favor. You can do so much, just by learning how to work around the lunar cycle and adjusting your actions accordingly.

Rather than fighting with the different moon phases, flow with them and understand what they mean. Comprehend how you must change your behavior and set your intentions exactly when the Moon is just beginning a new journey around the Earth. See why you should rest after completing each cycle and why it is of such great importance to recover, regain your strength, and start fresh. See how you can release anger and fear, letting go of any blockages that hinder your spiritual path. The universe is wise and perfectly balanced; you just need to find a way to align with the cosmos to supercharge your life!

Bathe under the moonlight and feel its energy surrounding you. Why would you settle for a life that is dependent on external factors, when you can take control of those factors and use them to find harmony in your life? Focus on your personal growth and walk steadily towards self-awareness. The Moon is your ally, as long as you let it work its magic. In this book you are going to find everything you need, so that you better understand the secrets of the Moon. There are abundant benefits in going with the flow of the cosmos, allowing the Moon to shine brightly into your existence, and changing your entire standpoint. Have faith in these glorious powers and trust in the universe, for it has been there forever.

Whether you have always dreamed of becoming a contemporary witch eager to cast your spells to promote your happiness, or you are just curious about your cosmic powers, this book will definitely enlighten you and fill you with gratitude about the world. I am sure you can't wait to start mastering the lunar secrets, so let's get started... I am wishing you the best of luck on this wondrous adventure that you are about to begin. Join me and let's shoot for the Moon!

❧ I ☙

MOON PHASE MASTERY: YOU ARE HOLDING THE KEY TO UNLIMITED POWER

The Moon is the absolute epitome of mysticism and romance, inspiring us ever since the dawn of ancient civilizations, and filling us with a transcendental sensation to cherish. As the Sun sets and darkness spreads across the world, it is the Moon that guides us along with thousands of stars scattered in the sky. People in love always turn to the Moon for help, for courage, and inspiration. They even resort to the Moon for guidance when all hope is gone, such as unrequited love or a condemned romance that cannot have a happy ending. But when the happy ending comes, it is the Moon that illuminates the most spectacular moments spent by those hopelessly romantic souls.

Every writer has found endless inspiration by gazing at the Moon and its different phases, while poets have created their best forms of literature motivated by its enchantment. Painters have dedicated their finest masterpieces to the Moon and the eerie atmosphere it so beautifully complements. Unlike the Sun, there is something unworldly about the Moon that makes it even more thrilling to look at.

Although we gaze at the sky every night, what we see changes in a pattern that allows us to dream away and imagine the secrets of our origins. It is a mystery we are all drawn to, in pursuit of conquering the truth and learning more about this astonishing element of the solar system.

Without a doubt, the Moon has played a great role in our culture and nature itself. The Earth would not be the same without its largest natural satellite orbiting around it, never stopping for a moment. What would happen if it did stop? The entire universe would be thrown out of balance, causing world-shaking events. Luckily, we can all rely on the Moon to maintain that precious balance and continue worshiping its mystical nature. We will continue celebrating its milestones, anticipating the glorious full moon, and observing the subtle silvery slivers as they form in the sky with each new moon.

Although the Moon is such a fundamental part of our very existence, the truth is that there are things about it we simply don't understand. In fact, many may think that the Moon stands still or that it is bright on its own. There are those who believe that some days the Moon simply doesn't appear in the sky, and others who do not realize that there is much more than what meets the eye in the various shapes of the Moon. In this chapter, I am going to show you what those moon phases really mean and how to interpret them. As soon as you unveil the mysteries of the Moon, you will gain knowledge that will enable you to fully comprehend the special power it holds. It is an exciting adventure, I promise!

UNDERSTANDING MOON PHASES

Why is the Moon visible on several days of the month in its full glory, whereas others you can barely see it? Well, unlike what many people might think, the Moon does not change shapes. It is always there, orbiting around the Earth and leaving its everlasting mark on us. So what happens? First of all, take a moment and think about the distance separating us from the blazing Moon: It is 35,000 kilometers away, floating in space, and offering mystical features and tantalizing beauty. What might come as a surprise is that the Moon itself is pretty dark! In fact, it resembles asphalt and it is equally reflective, too.

The Sun is responsible for illuminating the Moon, which in turn shines bright down on Earth. It is the Moon's strategic position exactly between the Earth and the Sun that allows it to glow like that! It is also spherical in shape and orbits around the Earth. So, the way we see it up in the sky every single day depends on where it stands at that time. On the bright side, literally speaking, the Moon is always half-illuminated by the Sun. It depends on the direction from which the Sun is shining over the Moon and the angle from which we get to observe from afar. The only thing that changes is the way we look at it from the Earth, causing those moon phases we all know and love.

Now, a full orbit of the Moon around the Earth takes about a month (29.5 days to be exact). As you can see, there is a striking resemblance between the words 'moon' and 'month', revealing that mystifying connection. So the beginning of the orbit represents the new moon. This is when the Earth, the Moon, and the Sun are all in alignment, and the Moon is as close as it can be to the Sun. As a result, the Moon is up during the day, although we cannot see it. At that point, we face the unlit half of the Moon and therefore we do not quite understand its presence in the sky. Sometimes, there might be a small silvery slice, but it is very subtle.

After a few days, we see that the Moon has traveled eastward, and it now allows us to see a crescent Moon. As the days go by, the crescent becomes bigger and bigger. This is what leads us to a "waxing crescent" Moon. After having covered one quarter of its orbit, the Moon is now about 90° away from the Sun. The 'terminator', meaning the line that divides the Moon in its illuminated and dark side, is now right in the middle. This might confuse you a little, as we have only covered the first quarter of moon phases. But as the Moon continues on swinging around, we move forward to the "waxing gibbous" moon phase. This is when the Moon appears swollen, hence the name.

Perhaps the most mind-blowing time of the Moon's orbit comes 15 days after the new moon. The Moon has now traveled half the distance of its orbit and now sits right opposite the Sun and the Earth. At that point, the Sun fully illuminates the side of the Moon and offers us one of the most amazing phenomena in the world. This is the "full moon" phase. Due to its position, the Moon now rises at sunset and sets at sunrise. The result is the astonishingly bright Moon we enjoy throughout the night. The full moon has inspired people for ages, and now you know how it is formed!

But then once again, the Moon continues on its course around the Earth and starts getting closer to the Sun. The same phases will take place, but in reverse. As the illuminated side becomes smaller, we enter the "waning gibbous" phase. The Moon is still shining brightly, but it slowly begins shrinking and its dark side gets bigger. A week after the full moon, the terminator is again slicing the Moon in two equal parts. We have entered the third quarter of the orbit, and in a few days we will observe the "waning crescent." Finally, after having traveled 360° around the Earth, the new moon is here, in anticipation of another thrilling lunar journey.

In Alignment With the Moon's Energy

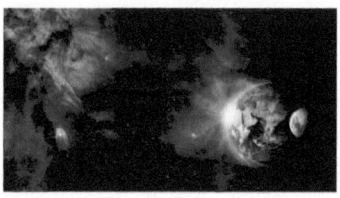

As the Moon orbits around the Earth, it controls its rhythms to a great extent. It is no secret that the Moon influences the water reserves on the planet, while the Moon's gravity causes the tides at sea (Choi, 2017). Take a moment and think of the analogy that we are made of water as well. So it makes perfect sense that the Moon influences humans on a deep, cellular level! This is a connection nobody can question; why you feel differently during the full moon, or any other phase of the Moon that has a direct impact on the universe.

The new moon offers an opportunity to set new intentions and start over again. It represents new beginnings, and there is so much potential that you can gain out of each new moon cycle. Recharge your body, mind, and soul under the omnipresent lunar power and get ready for what lies ahead! Even if you feel introverted, you should not worry! When the new moon comes, it is only natural that you seek some time alone to regain your strength, think about what has happened, and envision the future. Along with the waning crescent, setting new intentions becomes even more necessary. Plant the seeds of your dreams and wishes, so that you watch them grow. What would you like the universe to bring? What do you want to manifest in life? After having regained your strength, now you are ready to conquer what is yours by right!

In the first quarter, you may see some sort of resistance when it comes to the realization of your dreams and wishes. This should not let you down, as you now have the necessary power to overcome the obstacles and continue on your course toward accomplishing your intentions. Although there might be a few bumps along the road, this does not mean that you should give up or settle for less. The Moon is on your side, as long as you let it. Work hard and prepare to reap the benefits of your determination.

If need be, the waxing gibbous allows you the time to reassess and refine your actions accordingly. There might be times when the best thing for you is to modify your goals and set different intentions. Of course, no one is invincible and you should keep that in mind. Dreaming big is always a great thing, but at some point you must adapt to reality and make the most out of any situation. As the full moon approaches, you should be strategic and make sure that you harvest the fruit of what you have planted at the beginning.

During the full moon, things get tense and you may experience emotions that you cannot fully grasp or justify. Try not to get overwhelmed, because it is the lunar energy that drives them. Be open to receiving everything you have worked so hard to achieve during these past two weeks. This is the best time to watch those intentions come to life! At the same time, you will get new opportunities and you will realize that there are so many wonderful things for you to achieve. The world is filled with such potential and you need to be open to receive.

As the waning gibbous is formed, this is the time to feel the most grateful. You have already acquired what you wanted and you should be feeling extremely happy! Therefore, you should practice gratitude and express your positive emotions toward everything that has happened in your life. It has been an extraordinary journey and you have received abundance in all its forms, so now you must give thanks and share your enthusiasm with the world.

Any negative thoughts or bad events that have been dragging you down should be released. Let go and forgive others.

Do not hold on to any grudges, as something like that will poison you and eat you up from within. Instead, feel free to let go of your anger and do not consume your mind with such petty emotions. You should be looking upward, not downward! Finally, with the waning crescent you are free to surrender and take rest. This has been an intense lunar cycle, and you have benefited from its unique opportunities. You have received everything and now it is time to enjoy what you have acquired. Rest for a while, as a new cycle is about to begin with the new moon.

2

ACTIVATING YOUR POWER INFUSED ONENESS WITH THE MOON

Mankind has always been drawn to the Moon. Early humans observed this breathtaking celestial object in the sky and wondered what it represented. Philosophers looked at the Moon as the natural boundary between the Earth and heaven above. Our ancestors managed to determine the differences in nature according to the moon phases. This was monumental, as it enabled them to adjust to the distinct behavioral patterns of their prey, for instance. Consequently, humans were capable of surviving through the important findings that the Moon provided for them.

If you go back to Egyptian mythology, you will see that the Egyptians worshiped Khonsu. He was the God of the Moon, and his name literally translates to "the traveler" (World History Edu, 2020). This is a direct reference to the travels of the Moon, orbiting around the Earth. So, our ancestors had realized long ago that the Moon is not static, but instead moves in a continuous path that affects everything in the universe. Respectively, in Greek mythology, you will find Artemis, who is not only the Goddess of the Moon, but also the Goddess of wild animals and the wilderness as a whole. This reflects how ancient Greeks had also fully comprehended the immense impact of the Moon on all living things and nature itself.

Along with the Egyptians and the Greeks, ancient Babylonians managed to calculate the exact time it takes for the Moon to complete a full orbit around the Earth. More than that, they also took into account the slight orbit of the Earth around the Sun, and this is why their solar lunar calendars are so accurate! Incredibly, thousands of years ago, people were successful in determining what modern scientists would only calculate through the help of cutting-edge equipment and a wealth of knowledge stemming from observation. The Roman Goddess of the Moon is called Luna, revealing again how strongly the ancient civilizations believed in the power of the Moon.

When it comes to the weather forecast, the Moon can be of great help. When the Moon is high up in the sky, it affects the overall amount of rainfall. It does so by creating bulges in the atmosphere, which in turn interfere with the rain forecast (Hickey, 2019). Ever since antiquity, people have looked up in the sky and interpreted the Moon in order to identify several weather patterns. Since they used the Moon as a calendar, they marked its changes, and predicted how animals and nature as a whole would react. For instance, they saw the full moon as the time when animals would become more aggressive. This was a clear sign that they had to adapt, rather than miss out on the opportunity to outsmart their enemy.

It was a matter of self-perseverance for people back in the day to observe even the slightest changes in the lunar cycle, as well as any other changes in nature. This way, they managed to create a collective memory of the overall power of the Moon that was passed on to the newer generations. Although some of it might seem superficial or even superstitious, in reality it is the outcome of years and years of distilled observations. The Moon is much more than a centerpiece in the celestial decor and this is depicted in many cultural records that have survived throughout the centuries.

So we have already established that the Moon holds a special power over nature, and that this power has been made aware to humans even from the early days of civilization. However, what about humans themselves? What special power does the Moon hold over you and me? It makes total sense that we are also affected by the lunar cycle, but in what ways?

IMPACT OF THE MOON ON HUMAN BEHAVIOR

The Moon exerts gravitational force on everything in the universe. This includes the oceans, which explains why the Moon has an impact on the tides. Keeping that in mind, it makes absolute sense that the Moon holds a special power over humans. As well, we are mostly composed of water (up to eighty percent). What you should know is that the Moon's orbit around the Earth is completed in an elliptical pattern. This means that the two celestial objects do not have the same distance between them at all times. When they are closest together, this is called 'perigee.' On the other hand, when the Moon and the Earth are farthest apart, then this is called 'apogee.' The impact of the Moon on human behavior is directly associated with this very distance.

One more way in which the Moon affects human behavior is sleep. Maybe it is because on some days of the month, the Moon shines brighter and therefore alters our circadian rhythms. Be it as it may, no one can argue with the fact that some people are gravely affected by the Moon and get deprived of a restful sleep, especially right before or during the full moon. This of course is in perfect alignment with the moon phases, and particularly with the new moon offering an opportunity to rest and recover from the intensity of the entire lunar cycle (Grover, 2021).

The glow of the Moon is crucial, though, for the survival of several species. From sea creatures to deer and other animals, the lunar cycle offers a great way of knowing when to look for a mate, as well as when to go hunting. The tides of the sea can help move the eggs of some species to a safer environment. But how can the animal kingdom know? How do eels and corals, fish and turtles, reindeer and other mammals understand when is the right time? Do they have a built-in clock synchronized with the Moon and its phases? It seems that the Moon acts exactly like a signal, supercharging them and stimulating them to act as they do.

One of the main reasons why some ecosystems have been out of balance might be attributed to artificial light. Unlike the past, or any natural landscape away from the hustle and bustle of modern civilization, we have nowadays become accustomed to non-stop illuminated environments. However, there are many species out there that have absolutely no idea how to deal with these changes! They are thrown off guard and nature's balance is threatened. You might see it yourself, if you take a moment and really look at the world. In fact, you may even experience it in your own everyday life. Why do you find it hard to relax, sleep, let go? Why is stress so overwhelming?

Another connection that has remained controversial over the years is the menstrual cycle. Menstruation typically comes every 28 to 30 days, while the lunar cycle is completed every 29.5 days. As such, there is a time overlap between the two. If you take a moment and think about what menstruation represents, you will recognize that there is a new cycle of life celebrated every month. Those who menstruate can become fertile and bear the fruit of this fertility boost, before finally taking a rest and starting all over again. If you recall the lunar cycle, this is exactly what happens to the Moon. So there is definitely a bond between the two, at least conceptually.

If we get to think about it, there is a specific time in the lunar cycle when everything seems to blow out of proportion. Emotions can be magnified and people feel affected by something out of their control. This, of course, is the full moon, and a specific phenomenon that has inspired mankind, bringing a lot of conflict between those who believe in a deeper connection and those who remain skeptical. Which side are you on? Let's have a closer look at the impact of the full moon on us humans, putting emotions aside and focusing on what actually happens.

How About the Full Moon?

How often do you look up and marvel at the bright, full Moon? Are you convinced that it holds a special power over you, or do you believe that you are simply romanticizing this celestial phenomenon? You are not alone in this question! But over time, people have used this correlation to interpret signs and justify specific behavioral patterns. Have you ever watched wolves howling at the full moon? This is classically misinterpreted, since in reality wolves tend to howl even during the day, and follow a specific pattern. They look up in order for their howling sounds to spread further away, and in order to communicate with their pack more efficiently.

The full moon enhances everything that you already are, feel, and want. It heightens your senses and allows you to conceive things that would otherwise be too subtle to even realize. During the full moon, every trait of yours becomes magnified! Be it a positive or a negative attribute, it does not matter. What matters is that the full moon expands it and makes it more prevalent than it would otherwise be. At the same time, you may be feeling things too much. Yes, that's right; the full moon intensifies each and every single feeling! This is the reason you may feel saddened and filled with despair, without even knowing why. Anxiety, depression, as well as several mental illnesses spike during the full moon.

Since the Moon ultimately drives your emotions, it makes perfect sense why these emotions would be at their peak when the full moon approaches. We are biologically programmed to be affected by natural phenomena and this is one of the greatest in the world! As such, this is reflected in the way we feel and experience things. When you are in love, the full moon makes your heart beat faster and you long for moments of intimacy with your partner. When you are sad, you get even gloomier as the Moon gets brighter.

Maybe it has to do with our perception of the world. Since our senses are heightened and we are on alert, we turn to introspection. We take a look at our life and become more critical of it—disappointed even—when there is really no ground for such negativity. Perhaps it is the fact that we have been led astray from our true path that we get reminded of it at the full moon, which is extremely discomforting and fills us with self-doubt. In a time when nature gets in perfect alignment, we feel out of place. We feel like we do not belong and this is a rather disheartening feeling.

The full moon has been associated with lunacy ever since ancient times. In fact, this is why there is such a deep connection between the Moon (hence 'Luna' in Latin) and the disturbing mental state of being insane. Such people have been called lunatics, closely related to the Moon and its immense impact on human feelings and, ultimately, their actions. In the past, people believed that somehow the full moon made the world more aggressive and violent. They were convinced that crime rates increased dramatically at that time of every moment.

Even if such theories have been proven wrong over the

years, they still influence people. There is a strong cultural belief that the full moon wreaks havoc upon the world, leading to irrational behavior and promoting aggression, violence, and similar negative emotions. The full moon seems to have an impact on how we feel and this is not always a good thing! In the past, a lack of knowledge resulted in superstitions about the Moon, especially when it was the brightest in the sky. People watched animals more clearly during the night and therefore they thought that the full moon drove their behavior, enabling them to threaten humans. But it was most likely the other way around.

When a blanket of thick darkness covers everything around you, there is a lot that remains unseen. This does not mean that it is not there, it merely means that you cannot fully comprehend its presence. When the full moon comes, it unveils those mysteries of darkness and brings clarity.

❋ 3 ❋

WHAT ARE YOU WAITING FOR? HOW TO EASILY TRANSFORM YOUR LIFE WITH MOON PHASES

The Moon is the mother of the universe, representing the feminine power of the cosmos, whereas the Sun represents the masculine forces that infuse the world. These two are completely balanced, existing in perfect harmony with each other. The Moon enhances our bodily rhythms. During the dark or new moon, you can cast spells and set your intentions for a new beginning. If you wish to take a new path, this is the best time to schedule it! This is a productive time in the lunar cycle to sow the seeds of your ambitions, successes, and dreams, projecting them to the universe and allowing them to shape into reality.

Every lunar month depicts the time duration between two consecutive new moons. It is otherwise known as a "synodic month" and covers 29.5 days. There are people who mistake the synodic month for the "sidereal month." A sidereal month is a month that covers the time it takes for the Moon to circle the Earth, or 27.3 days. This is understandable because they both measure the same thing, practically. However, the sidereal month does not take into account the subtle orbit of the Earth around the Sun. This means that every time the Moon orbits around the Earth, it does so in an elliptical shape and that messes with the calculations a little. Consequently, the Moon has to move a little more each month to catch up with the Earth, leading to the synodic or lunar months.

With the new moon, this celestial object appears dark and empty. Gradually it gets filled up with light and brightness. Until you are completely illuminated by the abundant shining of the Sun, the Moon asks you to make the necessary changes to welcome this glorifying phenomenon up in the sky. You must generate light by yourself, so as to get perfectly aligned with the Moon and communicate with each other on a deeper level. This all happens in the period of the waxing moon, which is when the Moon increases its brightness and the surface that is covered with light. Put action into everything you wish to fulfill, and behold as you watch it unfold before your eyes. It takes some effort, but this effort is definitely worth it.

In the waxing moon, you should accumulate strength and make sure that you are on the right track. Extend yourself and prepare yourself for the most promising time of the entire cycle, which is three days prior to the full moon. You have already planted the seeds and now is the time to nourish them! Water them, so that they can grow and offer you their precious fruit during the full moon. It requires some time, so you should not get discouraged if a lunar cycle passes and you still have not reaped any fruit.

There will come a time when you benefit from your efforts! What you should focus on is the proper balancing aspect, though. Even if you put your whole heart toward achieving your goals, you must remember to rest and recover at the same time. It is not a sprint race you are training yourself for, rather than a continuous journey resembling a marathon. You risk feeling depleted and completely out of balance, drained of energy and determination. You do not want that, because you need your strength to claim what is rightfully yours!

During that time, there is an excellent 'pranayama' (practice of breath control) that you can follow! In this pranayama, you focus on sharp breaths through your nose. What you're aiming for is to get full contractions and releases in the abdominal area. When you inhale through the nose, the abdomen releases the air; when you exhale, the abdomen pulls in the air. The entire scheme should feel like a pump. You need discipline, in order to complete this, feeling the air in your lungs clearing your body and your mind. The more you do this pranayama, the more energized you will instantly feel.

Along with this pranayama, you can also do an energy 'mudra' (gesture) to succeed in your goals during the waxing moon. Touch the two middle fingers of each palm to your thumb, keeping the other three fingers stretched apart. Let those palms face upwards toward the sky and the Moon, while you close your eyes. In this way, you prepare yourself for new beginnings. You reset and get filled with energy, while also focusing on your intentions, and even getting clarity on what those intentions should be! It does not matter if you keep your hands at the level of your heart, or if you rest them on your thighs. This mudra works either way.

Visualize what you wish to accomplish in order to be able to project it to the world. Through this mudra, you concentrate on your goals and you clear the path for them to become reality. They will be fulfilled, as long as you remain on alert and pay attention to your needs, your desires, your dreams. You must have faith and nurture yourself, so as to embrace these new goals. Relax while you are keeping your eyes closed, picturing where you are after during this lunar cycle. You will feel heat generated, along with energy from within.

This is perfect, as it means that you're motivating yourself toward promoting these goals of yours! When you feel complete, bring your hands in front of your chest at heart level, palms pressed together. This is a gesture of gratitude, giving thanks to yourself. Just remember to do your pranayama and mudra daily during the waxing moon period, up to 100 exhalations at a time to achieve the optimal results. Calm down and visualize what it is you want, making space to put action into it, acknowledging that there will be challenges along the way.

There are moon cards available for you to buy and make use of, in order to maximize the effect of the Moon on your life. Once you purchase a moon deck, typically consisting of 44 cards, you can use them to set your intentions and remain focused on them. In fact, you have the option of using such cards to interact with your intuition, and developing a deeper connection to the universe surrounding you. Each card comes with its own mantras, as well as insights, and useful information that facilitates the whole understanding of the Moon and the universe.

FLOWING WITH THE DYNAMICS OF THE MOON

Women tend to be more in-tune with their emotions than men. Without a doubt, this is a stereotype that does not cover every single individual on Earth. However, it does hold some ground. Women and men, due to differing expectations, have learned to deal with feelings differently. Women are generally in deeper alignment with their feelings, and it may come easier to express themselves as individuals. It is worth noting that feelings stem from one's soul and they are genuine representations of your very existence. They offer a glimpse into the person's heart and mind, a glimpse of truth in an ocean of lies.

Emotions can be traced in the transits of the Moon on a person's chart. According to the specific place of the Moon every single day, or more accurately every single night, the person may experience turbulence in the way they feel. Since the Moon agitates the water element, it is responsible to a significant extent for the way we express our emotions. If you want to control your emotions, you need to learn how to grow a healthy relationship with the Moon and adhere to its powers. Mondays are supposed to be ruled by the Moon, as this is the day that highlights its energy! Therefore, this is the perfect time to fast, if this is something you're interested in. As a result, you will be in an elevated state of awareness. The same goes with the full moon.

One of the best mantras for the Moon is "Om Chandraya Namaha", which you can repeat 108 times or more to conquer its unique energy. In this way, you will be able to find a gateway to your very existence. As you will realize, the Moon represents so much in the world. First of all, it represents your mindset. This means that it reflects your thoughts and your own perception of your life. What do you believe about specific things? What is your opinion about several aspects of the world? Next, the Moon represents your mother and the relationship you have with her. Lastly, the Moon represents your home. The place where you feel secure and safe, your personal sanctuary of calmness.

So, the Moon is ultimately the Goddess of Light, Luna,

who drives you toward living a sustainable, fulfilling life. The Moon shines brightly upon you and offers you its mystical powers to expand your existence, and create the life you have always wanted. In order to achieve that, you must connect with Luna truthfully, without any obstacles getting in the way which prevent you from experiencing this special bond. You must do that consciously, with your whole heart and soul. Find a quiet place and create the perfect environment to promote the connection.

It is imperative that you create a sacred space where you can invite Luna to connect with you on that deep level. Unlike what you may think, there is an option for you to have such a place always available to you. No matter where you are, you can establish an etheric structure of light as a mobile sanctuary of light, connecting to the Moon regardless of any physical barriers present. If you want to activate this etheric structure of light, you must remain calm and be open in a receiving mode. Close your eyes and breathe deeply a few times, so that you can relax and let go of all tension.

Once you have come to such a state, you are ready to state what you want to create! More specifically, you can say something like this: *Temple of Moonlight, activate all around me. Below, above, up and down, create a safe sanctuary of light.* While you are saying this, visualize this sanctuary gradually forming around you. Allow enough space inside the structure in order to feel comfortable. It is archaic in shape, with tall pillars and radiating a purple color, emitting high frequencies. Imagine yourself surrounded by this magnificent sanctuary, and you will instantly feel like a huge burden has been lifted off your shoulders.

You can activate that temple on a daily basis, bringing it with you every single moment of the day and always keeping it available. Upon having established such a safe place, this is where you wish to invite Luna to connect with you. Do that and allow her to come in her human form: A woman, a radiant woman, that comes into your personal shelter and connects with you, shining her beautiful essence down on you and allowing you to become a part of her. As you continue on invoking her and getting to feel her close, you become more empowered and you feel that strong bond that has been created between the two of you. Indeed, this is a timeless bond beyond dimensions and it only grows stronger!

Interpreting the Past With the Power of the Moon

There are many people who feel haunted by their past lives. They sense that there is a deeper connection between what they are experiencing right now and what they have already experienced in their past lives. There seems to be a behavioral pattern, which is often attributed to karma. It is true that there are past experiences that form your behavior and channel you to make choices in life. No one can deny that humans are a species of habit. We are drawn by familiar things and this is why we seek uniformity, in order to feel safe. Intimacy is a wonderful aspect for us and therefore we tend to choose what we know over the unknown.

Take a moment and think for a while about yourself and the choices you have made so far in your life. Have they been based on a pattern? I presume you have understood by now that most of your decisions fall under the same principles, and you can somewhat predict what is going to happen in the future based on your past. Although this is not concrete and there is always the possibility of breaking the cycle, chances are that your actions are more or less aligned over time. You might feel threatened by that lack of originality, even though you may also feel relieved.

Karma is basically the notion of unresolved issues from past lives. So, based on what you have experienced before, you choose a life form and a path that is aligned with the past that allows you to maintain a specific course. According to evolutionary astrology, there are behavioral patterns that we seem to repeat no matter what in our lives. Even if these patterns are not beneficial to us, even if they hinder our progress and prevent us from experiencing life to its fullest potential, we still go ahead and make the same mistakes over and over again. Why would something like that happen? Why do we sabotage our lives?

The basic evidence of the existence of past lives lies within a simple yet indisputable observation: Imagine a girl who has grown up in a family where she suffered abuse. Her parents were alcoholics and had outbursts of anger. She grew up in a hostile environment, unable to establish safety and love. It is likely that she always felt out of balance, out of place, and she wanted a way out of this greatly discomforting reality. Although she grew up and became independent, she continued being drawn to those who resembled her parents in more ways than she could even admit to herself.

This feels like a pattern, like a self-fulfilling prophecy in the field of psychology. It is like you can almost foresee what bad thing is about to happen in your life, before even going down that road (Ackerman, 2018). The truth is that you feel comfortable in that pattern, because you have been used to it all this time. I am not referring only to your childhood and the early traumas you might have experienced at that sensitive period of your life. On the contrary, I am talking about all these past lives you have completed so far. Now you are conversing with the universe, asking for another try. This time you will do better, you will be better, you will tackle the challenges much more efficiently than before. Could there be more eloquent proof of past lives?

Now, let's try something cool that will tip you off as to how old you really are! Are you wise after having lived on Earth for countless years, or are you just setting out on your cosmic adventure? Do you want to find out how many lives you have had so far? Let's invoke the power of numbers, or 'numerology', in order to find out! First, get the number of the month when you were born. If it is a single digit, such as April, the 4th month of the year, simply keep this in mind. If it is December, the 12th month of the year, then add 1 and 2 together to get the number 3. Do the same with the day on which you were born. If you were born on the 2nd, you would get number 2. If you were born on the 14th, though, you would add the digits 1 and 4 to get number 5.

Finally, add the digits of your birth year and hold on to the number. For instance, those who were born in 1982 would get 1 plus 9 plus 8 plus 2. In other words, they would get number 20. Then, you are ready to find out the exact number of your past lives. Take the number of your birthday, your birth month, and your birth year together and add them. If you get 11, 22, or any digit from 1 to 9, then this is the total of past lives you have had so far. Otherwise, if you get any other double digit, add the numbers until you get a single digit. For example, if you come up with 42, then you should add 4 and 2 to reach 6, meaning you have had 6 lives so far.

4

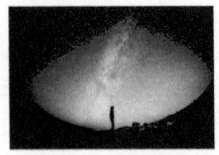

THE LAW OF ATTRACTION ON STEROIDS: MANIFESTING MASTERY WITH THE MOON PHASES

I am sure you are all familiar with the Law of Attraction: If you manifest positive thoughts and emotions, then the universe will return them to you. The same goes for negative emotions, however, so you should be extra careful as to what you project to the world (Lopez Simpson, 2017). The Law of Attraction is a magnificent concept, allowing you to receive all the blessings you want to see in your life, as long as you remain focused and have patience. Of course, the elements of nature play an important role in this process. The Moon is a celestial object holding extreme power, which makes it a great asset in your hands to manifest what you want to attract in your life.

Are you under the impression that you can only manifest during the full moon? Untrue! You are luckily able to do this throughout the lunar month, making use of the different phases to attract literally anything your heart desires! Luna, the Goddess of the Moon, is right by your side at all times. Even when you cannot see her, she is there guiding you to reach your highest self and live your life exactly the way you have always dreamed of. First of all, what makes it so special to manifest with the Moon? By now, you should know just how powerful the Moon is. Its energy is so unique, and therefore having the opportunity to use this magnificent power to supercharge your manifestations seems purely awesome!

Your spiritual self in collaboration with the eternal power of the Moon will definitely accelerate your manifestations, as long as you work around the moon phases and adjust your spells accordingly. In order to manifest with the Moon, all you need is proper time to dedicate to yourself. There is no need to rush into things, so you should find some time to concentrate solely on your manifestations. In addition, you should have a piece of paper or your journal throughout the entire process. Of course, you will need a pen or pencil to write with. If you wish to immerse in the calming experience of Moon manifestation, then some calming music in the background will work wonders along with some scented candles or incense.

It is great if you can combine the powers of the four elements into your manifestation. Obviously, by following my previous advice for burning candles or incense, you have the element of fire. Then, you can place windchimes to gather the element of the air into the room where you are about to manifest. For the element of water, a wonderful piece of advice would be to get a small water fountain, or make use of an essential oil diffuser. You can always add some ocean water to a cup or a bottle, or manifest while in the bathtub. Finally, you can capture the element of earth by bringing a plant or a rock in the room. Of course, you can always enhance your experience with the help of crystals and precious stones.

There are many other wonderful details that can make a difference in your manifestations. For instance, everybody holds some possessions that mean something special to them! A ring that has been passed on to you by your grandmother, a scarf that your best friend brought back from a cherished vacation, a picture of a loved one, or even the nostalgic aroma of your favorite cologne! All these elements can play an important role in your manifestation and can increase its power. Apart from that, you might feel creative and engage in putting together a vision board. There is nothing more stimulating than keeping everything neatly organized on a board, serving as constant reminders of what you wish to accomplish in life. Just let your imagination run wild! Use colorful markers, scraps from old magazines, post-it notes, paintings, and anything that makes sense to you! Turn to the vision board for inspiration and you will enjoy the energy boost every single time.

In my book, *Manifesting for Women*, I have delved into the mysteries of manifestations and I have included valuable information about how to meditate, journal, and practice gratitude and visualization in the most efficient manner possible. It would make me happy to see that you followed these guidelines towards reaching the highest levels of manifestation, and have received everything you have desired in life. I promise, there is so much more to this than a couple of affirmations and a journal! Once you play your cards right, you see how it all comes together and the results are purely mesmerizing. Your life has so much potential and it is a shame not to claim what you are entitled to experience. Just reach out, be open, and welcome this magnificent journey that has just begun for you.

WISHING ON THE MOON

Each phase of the Moon holds a very special power, and you should take advantage of these phases in order to make the most out of your manifestations. With the new moon, you know that you plant the seeds and you set the intentions for the entire lunar cycle. This is when you should write down what you want to happen in the next month, so that you project it to the world and the world responds back to you! It is important to remain calm and safe in your personal sanctuary. As the new moon starts its journey towards reaching fulfillment, you must focus on your wishes and manifestations. Be detailed and consistent, subtle yet conscious of your choices and be determined to make them real.

With the waxing crescent, just dig deeper and put some effort into those intentions. Work towards making them happen! This is not just wishful thinking and staying idle. On the contrary, you should put some pressure behind your entire endeavor and watch the magic unfold. Stick to your journal and make a list of those intentions, as detailed as they can be. This brings us to the third part of the lunar cycle, which is the first quarter of the Moon. At this point, you need to turn this list into an actionable plan. What can you do to forward your plan? Be strategic and think outside the box! Keep your mind on the end goal and make sure that you do everything within your power to accomplish that.

After doing all that hard work, we now shift over to the waxing gibbous phase of the Moon. Three days before the full moon arrives, you must get into a receiving mode. This is when you can use visualizations, so that you actually see how these intentions are going to look as they enter your life. If you are determined to rest more, then you can start visualizing the impact this rest is going to have on your body and mind. *See* your face radiating with glow, as you have just enjoyed a great night's sleep and you are filled with energy. *Feel* that rest taking over you and hold on to that feeling.

At last, it is the full moon and you have received what you have been waiting for throughout the lunar cycle. During the full moon, the energy is at its highest level and you want to take advantage of that any way you can! Upon receiving all those lovely intentions you have set at the beginning of this lunar cycle, you should now express your gratitude. You are thankful to the universe for what you have received, and you are especially thankful to the Moon for helping you achieve your success. It is now the time to sit down and write a gratitude list. Let go of any doubt that you may have been holding on to all this time, and as you let go, simply enjoy the abundance that has been brought into your life.

Now the Moon is beginning to go into the waning gibbous phase. This is the time to become conscious of what you have. Reflect on what you have accomplished so far. The waning gibbous phase is very important, as it allows you to see what you have been lacking. Assuming that you have not received what you wanted, there are certain limiting beliefs to blame. Now is the time to reveal these beliefs, so as to overcome them and pave the way for our next intentions. I know that you may be tense when you explore the fear and doubt that has been keeping you from accomplishing your goals. However, no matter how hard it might be for you, it is necessary that you look deeply into your most intimate places and find these limiting beliefs of yours. After all, they are undesirable and you do not deserve them.

During the next phase of the Moon, the third quarter, you can transform those limiting beliefs into your most valuable assets. This is a great feature, turning something negative into positive. "What doesn't kill you makes you stronger", to quote Friedrich Nietzsche (Wohns, 2020). Use the lessons that you have learned up until this moment and see the silver lining. Push forward, unleash your power, and watch yourself grow even further through these obstacles that you have been forced to overcome! Shift your focus and modify your behavior, so that the specific limiting belief you used to have does not touch you any more. Be careful, though, because you do not want to simply ignore the limiting belief. Hiding it under the rug just won't do you any good.

A mere 72 hours prior to the new moon, we have entered the waning crescent phase of the moon. You must have accumulated a lot of energy throughout this great adventure! In fact, it is highly likely that you are feeling a little overwhelmed by this process. So now is the time to empty all this energy and prepare yourself for the dark beginning of the new moon. Release the tension, let go of the manifestation you've created, and make room for the new intentions that you are going to sow in a few days. You may hold on to the precious experiences, but you must release all the energy that you have put into it. Otherwise, you would feel exhausted and you would have no will to start over.

The new moon represents rebirth. In absolute harmony with one's menstrual cycle, this is the exact time when you will begin a new journey towards creating a new life. Even though the new moon is dark, there is an illuminated side of the Moon always shining bright in the universe! It is up to you to wait until it is revealed to you once more. Remember that your intentions should be clear and honest, coming from the depths of your soul, reflecting who you want to be and what you want to do at any given time. You should only focus on what actually matters to you and no one else. This is your life, so you must paint it in your own true colors.

Whatever you do, it is important that you practice gratitude and thank the universe for your blessings. In today's world, many people forget to do that, and they believe they are entitled to everything without giving anything back. Nothing could be further from the truth, however. The laws of the universe are everlasting and omnipresent, governing the planets and celestial objects, humans and all living creatures. We are only a tiny fragment of this universe and we are expected to cohabitate in harmony with the rest of the world.

It is a matter of understanding who you really are and what you are meant to do in the world. The universe will listen to your calling, but will only respond to those who appreciate what they receive. If you wish to be abundant in life, you need to give thanks for all the prosperity that comes your way, while appreciating the fact that you have been blessed with so many things. Do not forget or underestimate the importance of gratitude. By doing so, you comprehend the very essence of the world and deeply realize the core of existence. You are meant to be happy, but you ought to understand how fortunate you are, and show your respect, your gratitude, your thanks towards the eternal powers of the universe.

Sometimes we get discouraged by the fact that our intentions are not successful during the lunar cycle. I have heard over and over again from people that the Moon might not be as powerful as they had initially anticipated. They do not understand that the universe truly sees inside you, and does not grant your wishes unless they come straight from the heart. Moreover, there are intentions that are far more complicated than others. As such, it will require more time for these intentions to be turned into reality. In this case, what you need to do is be patient and welcome change as it is formed.

Following the moon phases, before the lunar cycle ends, you must show the Moon how appreciative you are of what you have received throughout the month. It doesn't matter if you have successfully achieved your goals or not. Each cycle offers unique lessons, and you need to keep your eyes open in order to acquire that precious knowledge that will serve as future wisdom. For instance, you may have discovered what has been holding you down in the form of limiting beliefs. What has prevented you from pursuing your career ambitions so far? Who has been pulling you down, discouraging you from actually realizing your dreams and desires?

Be truly passionate about manifesting! Believe it in your

core that you are destined to succeed, and this is exactly what you are going to do. Unless you set your intentions with that in mind, you cannot expect them to be brought to life. The universe needs to know that you are strongly energized about these intentions in order to program their realization. Through passion and commitment, you build your armor and you show the world how much you want to attract all these marvelous things into your reality. After all, when you believe that you already have that abundance in your life, your frequencies become elevated and this is projected to the universe around you.

Let's Talk About Love

Love makes the world go round, right? Who could ever imagine a world without love, without affection, without that unique bond between two people that defies dimensions, expectations, and limitations? That uplifts your spirit and creates a bond that cannot be broken? One who has not yet been loved has not yet realized the beauty of being alive. I know that romance has been praised throughout the years, and we have all grown up waiting for the moment when we would meet that unique person who would connect all the missing pieces. For when we meet that person, our life would then make sense, and we would have the perfect reason to enjoy every single moment together.

For some, this all sounds idyllic, and sometimes people stop believing in love. They are either too afraid to let go and trust others, or they feel that they do not deserve to spark such intense emotions. Of course, everyone deserves to love and be loved. When you meet that person who you have been waiting for all this time, you cannot stop giggling and you feel butterflies in your stomach! The world is finally smiling back at you and you can look forward to even more wonderful moments ahead. Who wouldn't want to welcome pure bliss into their soul?

Yet, along with love comes heartbreak, jealousy, unrequited love, and pain, like you have never experienced before. The intensity of emotions is earth-shattering and makes many people swear that they will never love again. They feel an emptiness that resembles no other, and grief after the loss of someone dear. How can they cope after such an immense change? Many choose to remain numb, shying away from even the slightest form of love that might make them feel something again. Of course, others may choose to stay in the game and continue on their journey towards finding true love.

Whether you have already found your significant other or you are still looking, it goes without even saying that love is always in the air. It doesn't matter if you choose to ignore it, love's dynamics are simply too intense. Obviously, you can manifest love into your life or you can improve your current relationship through moon rituals. Nature is by your side; all you need to do is ask. But before moving forward with the specific moon rituals that can bring you closer to your love interest, you must realize that it all boils down to your relationship with yourself.

No matter how frequently you do those rituals, unless you fully comprehend that a loving relationship starts from within you, chances are that you will never experience it. If I were to ask you right now what love means for you and what the first thing that comes to mind about love is, what would you answer? If the answer is a specific person, then you may need to make a shift in your mindset. You should focus on yourself, because otherwise you may be sabotaging yourself, and you would be hindering your progress towards finding that true love.

In a way, your romantic partner is the mirror of your deepest self. Even though it is easier to believe that you are not getting the love you need because another person is not giving that to you, the real culprit is yourself. Once you dig a little deeper, you will see that your relationship (or the lack thereof) is a reflection of the way you hold the love energy from within you. In fact, your entire existence is the reflection of your inner energy pattern. If you believe deep inside that you are not worthy of being loved, then what you get in real life is a manifestation of this belief. It is awful, but it is the truth. Of course, this does not affect your possibility to create superficial relationships. As soon as the relationship tends to get more serious, your insecurities and feelings of worthlessness emerge.

I hope you are determined to reverse that situation and allow yourself to be loved. In order to do that, I want you to take a piece of paper or write down in your journal all these things that you would expect your significant other to offer in your relationship. For instance, you can write: *I want my partner to bring me flowers*, *I want my partner to talk sweetly to me*, *I want my partner to express how proud they are of me*, or even, *I want my partner to love me unconditionally, without judgment*. All these things reflect how you want others to treat you and especially the person you love the most.

Well, having completed the list, it would be good to go over it and read each and every single thing that you have written. Once you do, start treating yourself like the partner you desire. Show yourself the love that you deserve, the love that you are entitled to in life. Start buying flowers, take the day off, go out for a spa treatment, stroll leisurely down the park, and watch your favorite movie. Do whatever makes you happy, so that you feel loved—by you! This is the secret to unlock unconditional love by others.

One more thing that you need to remember is that there is a cosmic timing for everything to happen... and the universe knows it! Even if you are in a hurry and want to meet the love of your life right away, this might not be the right, divine timing for you. As an entity, you are much bigger than what your mind is able to understand. You are part of the universe and therefore you should adhere to its rules, waiting for the perfect timing to come. I can sympathize with the concept of wanting something to happen right now. However, you should control your urges and resist that feeling of despair. This is now who you are deep inside.

What you want to manifest should come to you effortlessly, as part of the natural flow. Take a moment and think of all the times you got what you really wanted. If you look carefully, you will see that more often than not, you were not even paying attention! You did not pursue what came your way, but you welcomed it as an unexpected gift. It took you by surprise and this made you feel even more wonderful. How many times was this a manifestation of your urges? How many times did you think: *Oh I must have that NOW!* and the universe responded immediately by giving it to you? I am guessing that this has never happened in your life, as it has not happened in mine either.

When it comes to moon love rituals, you should work around the lunar cycle and take advantage of the different phases. The new moon of every month is the time when the Sun and the Moon are in conjunction. They are together, creating a divine portal that enhances the actual power of your manifestations. So during the new moon, you should clear your mind, rest, and meditate. Focus on the present moment, appreciate it, and then write down a list of your desires. Remember that you need to project these desires in a positive manner. Rather than saying, *I want this person to love me*, you should say, *I am an expression of divine love and I am worthy of being loved.*

As soon as you have this list complete, you should keep it somewhere safe and protected. You can choose to put it in an altar, on your bedside table, or even within your daily journal. After a fortnight, there will be a full moon. This is the time when the Sun and the Moon are actually opposite to each other. Similarly to the new moon, this is also a very powerful time during the month. Whatever seed you have planted now is going to flourish. So, you need to be careful and look out for those manifestations of your set intentions. If you don't see anything, then you must search for blocks that hinder your progress.

A full moon ritual also involves meditation. You should pick a nice and quiet place, bathed by the light of the full moon. Sit comfortably with your palms on your knees facing upwards. Start breathing deeply, inhaling the divine love and exhaling those blocks that stand in the way. After completing this full moon ritual, you can write a list of everything that you would like to acquire during the full moon. Have another look at your new moon desires and see what has manifested into your life. Be very open and flexible, as this is a never-ending process. Sometimes it takes a lot more lunar cycles for an intention to become reality. This is the beauty of life, so embrace it and cherish every moment!

HOW TO DROP JAWS AND SAY "I TOLD YOU SO" WITH LUNAR FUELED SUPER-ABILITIES

Are you interested in skyrocketing your intuition, predictions, and psychic abilities with the help of the different moon phases? I am sure you are! It is a fascinating journey around the cosmos that can boost your manifestations and welcome those gorgeous intentions into your life. You simply need to know where to look. The Moon is a powerful celestial object, influencing the Earth on so many levels. It governs the unconscious realm and intuition is part of that. Your intuitive mind is a sacred gift and the Moon allows you to connect with it deeply and strongly.

We are parts of nature, so it is only fair to assume that we are also affected by its magnificent power. However, how can you supercharge your abilities and increase the odds of inviting absolute bliss into your life? As the Moon orbits around the Earth and reflects the spectacularly abundant light of the Sun, it becomes a portal channeling vast energy. As soon as you understand how this energy is distributed throughout the lunar cycle, you will be able to maximize its effectiveness on both yourself and those around you. You will be capable of controlling your emotions and allowing them to flow naturally, as your intuition is speaking to you through them. If you are determined to delve into the mysteries of the cosmos and change your life based on the power of the Moon, then you need to interpret those signs, see when to act, and when to stay still.

First of all, let's focus on an essential part of everyday life. Intuition is directly linked to your personal happiness and self-actualization. It is an important aspect of your personality, driving you to act the way you do. This is what drives you to live life to its fullest potential, taking advantage of the opportunities that it has to offer. How can you trust your intuition, though? How can you be certain that it is not just your impatience trying to take over, leading you to catastrophic events of great proportions? With the guidance of the Moon, trusting your intuition will be exactly like returning home.

Intuition can be described as your inner voice, your gut, or that feeling of knowing something beyond a shadow of a doubt. This voice from deep inside you is attempting to speak to you, advising you as to what you should do. It is worth mentioning that intuition barely adheres to social norms or other rules that have been dictated by the world. It is that higher self of yours who is trying to communicate with you! Even if you are afraid to let go, it is in your best interest to reconnect with that part of yourself that has remained dormant all this time, due to those norms and other rules applied to you by society.

So as you can see, most people have neglected nurturing their intuition and truly realizing that it is there to guide them. Your goal should be to learn how to distinguish your inner voice—your intuition—and listen to what it has to say. Another interesting point of view is that this voice also represents your ancestors guiding you, motivating you to push forward and become the best version of yourself! This is a wonderful notion, and is based on the eternal wisdom of the collective that is translated into your intuition. Through this voice, you are expected to break free from a vicious cycle that keeps you restrained and limits your potential.

I completely understand why there is so much doubt associated with listening to one's intuition. Since misinterpreting that voice happens more frequently than what I would like to admit, people get skeptical. They are critical of intuition, and some might even question its overall value in a person's life. Nevertheless, intuition is your constant motivator to progress and become the best version of who you really are. You should not underestimate its importance, as it is the fuel that sparks your existence and allows you to achieve greatness!

If you are concerned about whether or not to listen to your intuition, there are several things that you can do. Trust the power of the Moon and adjust your rituals according to the specific moon phases. This way, you will get optimal results. First and foremost, you can communicate with your deeper self through meditation, especially during the full moon. Meditate with the intention of giving space to your inner voice and discovering that intuition deep inside you. Whether you are at home in your personal sanctuary or outdoors, you can meditate after creating the perfect atmosphere. As we've discussed, you are more than welcome to burn some sage or light a scented candle, use wind chimes or listen to the therapeutic sounds of the waves, the wind, or water flowing.

After having created such a marvelous, welcoming atmosphere that promotes relaxation and enables you to feel comfortable, you can start asking yourself questions about yourself. For example, you can ask, *Who am I? How am I feeling now? Why am I unhappy today?* and similar questions that pop to your mind. Now, before any social monitoring takes place, your intuition is going to step up and answer. So once you hear your deeper self answering those questions, you know that you are communicating with your intuition. This is best performed in the new moon, when you set your intentions for the lunar cycle that has just begun.

You can do the same with any issue that has been troubling you for ages, such as, *Should I quit my job? What career path should I follow? Is my relationship healthy?* and so on. These are just a few of the questions that you can ask yourself to establish your connection with your inner voice. I am sure that you may feel a bit awkward at first. This is perfectly understandable, because you have never been encouraged to rely on that voice in your life! But if you ease yourself into the process and take some time, this will all flow naturally.

Besides meditation, you can also try getting out of your comfort zone! Set out on an adventure on your own and listen to what that inner voice has to say. Listen to that voice and do what it tells you to do, in order to evaluate the results at the end of the day. Chances are that you will have achieved something out of the ordinary, something that has made you feel great about yourself. Last but not least, indulge in art, but remember to avoid any agenda. For instance, take a piece of paper and a pen (or a pencil) and start free writing. Do not think about it; just let those words flow naturally. Try abstract painting, freestyle dancing, or whatever works for you.

Through these amazing activities, you can get in touch with your intuition! Explore the powerful effects the Moon has on your own existence and delve into its presence deep inside you! Be gentle and do not beat yourself up if you do not succeed in listening to your gut right away. It may take a few lunar cycles to open up and prepare yourself to accept this mental shift, to embrace your most creative, intuitive, and emotional self. All those years you have suppressed its intensity and this is why it has remained hidden in the darkness, shying away from communication. Remember to avoid all judgment, and do your best to feel like a child again. Perhaps this was the only time when you were in absolute alignment with your intuition, as no social norms got in the way and prevented you from listening. Don't worry, you will get there!

PREDICTING THE DIFFERENT MOON PHASES

How can you be certain when it comes to the specifics of a lunar cycle? How can you tell, beyond any doubt, that tonight it is the waxing crescent phase, or that three days from now there will be a waning gibbous phase? Well, there is always the internet and no one can argue that *Google is your best friend*. Going online, you can easily use any interactive tool that allows you to identify the exact phase of the Moon on that particular day! For instance, you can see that the Moon is at four percent of a waning crescent upon looking it up (Sinnott, 2017). These tools are highly accurate, and they can even help you go as far back in the past as you wish for a deeper understanding of lunar cycles.

Even though technology has come a long way and you can get that type of information effortlessly, it is much better if you figure out yourself how to calculate the phases of the Moon. You already know that the Moon orbits around the Earth on a monthly basis, and this is the reason why there are such differences in the way we look at it from afar. This is an elliptical orbit, meaning that it is not one hundred percent circular. On the contrary, we also learned that there is a mild imbalance in the circle, and this leads to 29.5 days instead of the actual 27.3 days that it would take the Moon to orbit around the Earth in full cycle.

However, when you want to calculate the moon phases in the sky, you take into consideration that a full lunar cycle lasts 28 days. As we have seen, the actual cycle does not last 28 days, so take this with a grain of salt. Now, what you want to do is depict this cycle on a piece of paper. So, draw a circle and cut it into four equal slices, just like you would do with a pizza cutter. Then divide those pieces in two. In this way, you will get a full circle with eight equal pieces that you can number. Guess what? These are the lunar phases for you to remember.

If you want to have a clear perspective of this lunar cycle, then imagine cutting the circle into two with a horizontal line. Since the entire cycle lasts 28 days, it is only logical that half of it will be 14 days. So a full moon, which is number 5 in the numbered cycle on your paper, will take place exactly 14 days after the new moon. Respectively, if you are at number 2 (the waxing crescent phase) and you want to calculate where you are going to be in 14 days, then the answer is 6, or else the waning gibbous phase.

You may want to calculate where you are going to be in seven days' time. This is of course easy to predict as well, since what happens is that a lunar cycle will have moved a quarter of its course within seven days. Unlike what you might think, not all phases have the same duration! In this case, number 1 is the new moon and lasts for a single day. After that, there is the waxing crescent that lasts for six days. So upon reaching the eighth day of the lunar cycle, you will have reached the first quarter, or number 3. In a similar pattern, you can also calculate where you are going to be after 21 full days in the cycle.

Obviously, over time this gets easier to understand, and you become much better at predicting the various moon phases. Typically, with the help of this visualization of a cycle divided into eight equal slices, you will always be able to identify which phase you are on, and which phase you will be on in a time period of 7, 14, 21 or 28 days. Nevertheless, there are several other cool techniques that can aid you in your attempt to interpret nature and its marvels. Whether you are experienced in this, or you are a complete novice, you can work wonders with the right tools.

If you do not want to get into all that fuss, and assuming that you just do not care for visualizing the cycle in your mind, you can refer to a ping pong ball. To be honest, any white object in a spherical shape will do, as long as you can hold it in your palm. So go outside and look up in the sky on a clear day, approximately an hour before sunset. You will have the opportunity to spot the Moon then. What you need to do is hold the ping pong ball up to the sky, right next to the Moon. Since the Sun illuminates the ball from the same angle as it does the Moon, you will instantly see the specific moon phase depicted on the ball.

Are you more of a visual person? If so, then you can use your creativity and whip up something truly amazing! At the same time, your craft may help you get a better glimpse at the moon phases. You are going to need a white styrofoam ball and some black paint. Your next step is to paint half of the styrofoam ball black. While that dries, write down the different moon phases on a piece of cardboard or construction paper as they occur in a monthly cycle. Then, glue the styrofoam ball onto the center. When you glue the styrofoam, just make sure that the black side faces the new moon phase.

According to each phase, you can see the illuminated parts of the Moon appear in perfect harmony.

Slightly less complex than that, but equally inspiring, is the following method to predict the moon phases with great accuracy: You will need a white styrofoam ball again in order to complete your experiment. This time, the ball needs to be placed on top of a pencil or a straw. Use a lamp with a bright light to represent the Sun. The styrofoam ball will once again be the Moon. Once you stand facing towards the lamp, the illuminated part of the styrofoam ball that you are holding in your hands that represents the Moon is behind you. Therefore you cannot see it. Instead, you see the dark part of the Moon. Having that as a starting point, move in a circular manner and watch the different moon phases as they unfold on the ball.

Finally, you can create a moon slider to identify the exact moon phase you are on every single day. Use thin cardboard or construction paper and cut a large square, which you then fold in half When you unfold this, you will have a right and a left side. Make sure your cardboard or paper is relatively big,, because your next step is to draw the eight different moon phases. These drawings will be your point of reference. Identify the moon phases as you complete the drawings. Then, cut out a small circle in the middle of your circle. This is going to be your Moon! It is best if you use white or light-colored paper to construct the whole craft.

After doing this, you will need to get a black piece of paper. On one half, cut out the shape of a large circle, and on the other side, cut out a crescent. As the lunar cycle begins, place the black paper over your white paper, so that it covers the entire circle. While the Moon orbits around the Earth, watch its reflection in the sky and move the black paper to match that picture. The only limitation with this method is that you cannot depict the first and last quarter. Fortunately, they are quite easy to remember even without this special craft. So this is another technique on how you can tell which moon phase you are on without fail!

What Are Your Psychic Gifts Defined by the Stars?

Do you want to know what your psychic abilities actually are, based on your Moon astrology birth chart? There are many more than just a few, well-known traits attributed to you by your sign. In fact, there are amazing psychic gifts that the stars and the Moon shower down to you according to your exact birthday! Below, I am going to analyze those psychic abilities that you have been blessed with at the time you were born. Read along and see if these characteristics connect with you!

First of all, Aries comes with a fiery intuition. It is, after all, a zodiac sign representing the element of fire! You have been given the power to sense the perfect timing to start something fresh, and take chances and risks. Your intuition is definitely spot-on and allows you to modify your actions towards achieving your goals in the best manner possible. However, at some point, this intuition of yours might be mistaken with lack of patience. If you feel that you just cannot wait any longer, which makes you rush into a specific action, then this is probably a trait you must tame and try to control.

Representing the earth element, Taurus is able to rationalize things and remain stable. Being grounded gives you the best perception about everything that happens in your life, enabling you to avoid negative consequences that often stem from impatience and acting on the spur of the moment. Your psychic power has to do with a deep connectivity between yourself and your surroundings. You listen to the environment, and you get to decide how to act based on what you make of the situation at hand. Take a moment and think about the energy you get upon entering a specific room. This is your psychic gift projected to you, so do not ignore it.

Moving on to Gemini, here the element of air is omnipresent. Geminis are often clairvoyant, as they are gifted listeners and communicate with the universe on a deep, genuine level. You feel like your mind never ceases to function, which is absolutely right! Thousands of images literally pop into your mind non-stop, while your eagerness to learn and process every single detail enables you to channel spiritual messages. You are great at communicating with others, which offers you the opportunity to be creative and indulge in writing, speaking, and consulting.

Cancer reflects the element of water. It is a highly sensitive zodiac sign, meaning that you probably feel that you are overwhelmed by emotions at specific times within the lunar cycle. For instance, during the new moon, Cancers will feel the collective emotions flowing through them and charging them greatly. You have a special ability to connect to others' feelings and this makes you a great listener, as well as a unique person to empathize with. However, there are times when this gift seems to be overpowering you. This is when you need to remember that it is actually a gift and it is meant to heal others in moderation.

Returning to the fire element, now is the time for Leo to shine! What is so intriguing about this sign is the fact that it holds a deep connection not only with the Sun, but also with the Moon. It is the perfect combination of a dynamic personality, with great courage and determination, which at the same time attracts people with the magnetism of the Moon. So your psychic gift is none other than your charisma, your unique blend of attributes that makes you irresistible! You channel positive energy and people get inspired through your presence. Spread that energy into the world, because this is your calling.

Virgo is the second zodiac sign representing the earth element. You have the psychic power to be present in the moment and pay attention to the slightest of details. Even though some might claim that you always opt for perfection, you also remain grounded and communicate with the world in its very core. A great thing about Virgo is that they can tap into the divine knowledge and integrate it into the world. As a result, you can manifest ideally and you can use this psychic gift to naturally heal others. It is an amazing opportunity to bring the vastness of the universe into the three-dimensional world we live in.

Next, Libra is another sign ruled by the element of air. Libras are people who crave balance and do everything within their powers to smoothen any differences. They are able to see past the polarity that oftens leads to conflicts, since they realize the value of balance and harmony. Your psychic gift is to integrate dualities and bring balance to the world, appreciating the unique aspect of every single view. Upon recognizing a conflict, your natural instinct dictates that you resolve it without delay. You value the opposites and do not try to change anything, rather than only seeing the good and focusing only on that.

Scorpio is another water-ruled sign. In this case, you can see right through people and understand what they are actually made of. You cannot be fooled, since you are greatly intuitive and you read the energies quite naturally. To that extent, more often than not, a Scorpio will go away and try to hide from the rest of the world. They do not wish to reveal what has been revealed to them by others, as this might feel too intense. Furthermore, Scorpios are extremely sensitive and deep as a sign. This is why many become mediums, communicating with other dimensions. Besides looking out for yourself, since you are very vulnerable, you also need to realize your boundaries regarding spiritual trespassing.

Another fire sign of the zodiac is Sagittarius. If you have a Sagittarius Moon, then you most likely never lie about anything in your life. It is true that Sagittarians do not feel the need to hide things or mislead others. On the contrary, they are ruled by an immense feeling of optimism and they tend to light up the room as soon as they enter. You will find it extremely easy to manifest great things into your life, as your high vibrational frequencies allow you to do that easily. Your imagination runs wild and you are capable of vibrant visualizing. In addition, you motivate others and bring out the best in them.

Capricorn is another earth sign. Your psychic gift is that you are able to remain focused and determined in a single thing, away from any distractions. You are extraordinarily passionate about what you want to do and do not rest until you have succeeded. As a consequence, you are the best manifester in the entire zodiac! You have been blessed with a sense of deep, absolute knowledge as to what you must do in order to bring those manifestations into your life. By exuding such wisdom and maturity, you often become a role model or a mentor to others.

Moving on to Aquarius, there is a contradiction here. Although this is an air sign, it is represented by the water bearer. How cool is that? By fusing those elements together, you create an electric atmosphere. You are naturally connected to the universe, to what lies beyond. Your psychic power enables you to understand what happens in the world on a deeper level and comprehend the truth behind the lies. Because of your connection to the eternal power of the universe, you often astral travel or daydream. Finally, you have the ability to foresee the future and read through other peoples' intentions.

Wrapping up the zodiac sign, Pisces is indeed the last water sign, and comes with great mysteries waiting to unfold.

You are also greatly intuitive and you are in tune with the beyond. Your psychic gifts are relevant to your sensitivity. Because of your extreme receptiveness, you often get overwhelmed by the intensity of the emotions and you tend to try and escape. You feel what others feel and you experience clairvoyance. Moreover, you have deep compassion for others. If you have a Pisces Moon, you are introverted and shy.

6

WHAT THEY DON'T TELL YOU ABOUT ZODIAC SIGNS

What sign are you? is much more than a convenient line to start a conversation! Obviously, your zodiac sign has a great effect on your life. Whether you care to admit it or not, the planets have aligned in a unique pattern on your birthday and they have shined down on you their special powers! Floating in the sky in a perpetual dance with the stars and the other magnificent celestial objects, the planets have created a wonderful flow of energy and they have been imprinted on your existence forever.

Due to the complexity of the solar system, you cannot expect that a single planet or star affects you all on its own. On the contrary, there is an entire system that forms this sophisticated structure that allows you to grow and expand. As soon as you become aware of its power, you will be able to interpret your birth chart and understand how astrology defines who you really are. It is astonishing to see just how much you have been influenced by the stars, the planets, the houses, and the specific positions of each and every single celestial element!

Below, you will have the opportunity to analyze your natal chart and learn more about the details that you should pay attention to. Get a journal and start creating the foundations on which you are going to unveil all those mysteries of the universe... they all start with your zodiac sign!

HOW TO READ YOUR ASTROLOGICAL CHART

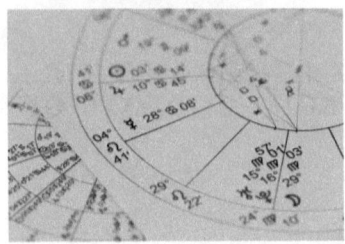

Unless you become familiar with the various celestial elements, you will never be able to fully grasp the magnitude of astrology. As a result, you will be constantly missing out on the marvels of the universe! If you are determined to understand how the Moon works and what effect it has on you throughout the lunar cycle, you must also pay attention to the planets and other celestial objects that surround the Moon and interact with it on various levels.

You do not have to be a professional astrologer, in order to comprehend astrology and its basic concepts. To help you, I have gathered here everything you may need to read and interpret your astrological chart. Below is all the information that allows you to delve into the mysteries of your birth chart, and understand how the planets, the signs, and the houses interact with each other. This is a wonderful collaboration—a planetary symbiosis if you will!

Before moving on, I highly recommend that you get a piece of paper or your journal, and a pen or marker to keep notes. First, divide your paper into three tables. You will have a column dedicated to the planets, another one to the signs, and a third one devoted to the houses. Now, you must be careful when you complete this chart. It is imperative that you write down everything in order, so that each planet is aligned with a sign and a house. Begin by writing down the Sun. This is an all-mighty planet that governs the sign of Leo and the fifth house. Of course, feel free to draw the Sun next to the word or scribble the zodiac sign next to its name!

Below the Sun, you get the Moon. The Moon governs the sign of Cancer and the fourth house. Continue writing down the planets on your table, keeping in mind that the following planets rule more than one sign: Mercury rules both Gemini in the third house and Virgo in the sixth house. In a similar pattern, Venus rules both Taurus in the second house and Libra in the seventh house. Now, something even more impressive happens with the next three planets: They rule one sign and they co-rule another! Does that sound confusing? Maybe a little bit! But you can use your chart to make it as straightforward as possible!

To be more specific, Mars rules Aries in the first house. At the same time, it co-rules Scorpio along with Pluto in the eighth house. Jupiter rules Sagittarius in the ninth house and co-rules Pisces along with Neptune in the twelfth house. Last but not least, Saturn rules Capricorn in the tenth house and co-rules Aquarius with Uranus in the eleventh house. By planning this out, you can have a chart with all the analogies readily available for you to use any time you want to learn something about the universe.

Another thing you need to remember when you read your astrological chart is the longitude and latitude. There are four points in the chart that you should highlight. More particularly, you get the 'IC' in the fourth house. This is short for "Imum Coeli" or "the bottom of the sky." It is also called the "midnight point" and focuses on your roots, as well as your inner self. 'DC' stands for the 'Descendant' and it is positioned in the seventh house. It is the western angle of the horoscope and determines all you need to acquire before you are able to grow and expand your existence.

'AC' is short for 'Ascendant', and it is located in the first house. Also known as the "rising sign", this sign ascends on the eastern horizon and represents everything that you truly are! The AC is essentially your identity, both your appearance and what lies within you and forms your personality. Completing these four angles, you get the 'MC' in the tenth house. This is short for "Medium Coeli", or 'Midheaven.' The MC is located at the highest point of your astrological chart and reflects your personal success. It shows the world your purpose in life and leads you to your higher self.

Besides these fundamental elements in the birth chart, you should also leave some space for extras. You can use a different page or leave a specific place on top of the chart where you can write these additional elements that will help you interpret the celestial world much more efficiently. In this category, you need to include 'Chiron.' It is located between Saturn and Uranus, always moving in an elliptical orbit. In Greek, Chiron means the "Wounded Healer." This is a marvelous asteroid, rather than a planet! It holds special power and it represents those aspects in your life that have always felt more challenging, leaving you wounded in a way.

In these extras, you should definitely include "Black Moon Lilith" as well. This is not an object or a planet, but more of a specific point. What is amazing about Lilith is that it reflects your impulses without any agenda or filter. It is your deepest, rawest, most primitive form of desires, along with the darkest side of yourself that emerges through this point in the astrological chart. Of course, you should also add four more asteroids in these extra elements of your natal chart! These elements are 'Pallas', 'Juno', 'Vesta', and 'Ceres.' Pallas is Goddess Athena in Greek mythology, the Goddess of wisdom and warfare. Juno is the Goddess of marriage and commitment in Roman mythology. Vesta is the Goddess of home and hearth, while Ceres is the representation of motherhood!

Apart from all that, there are two extremely important elements that you must include: The North and South Nodes of the natal chart are points located right opposite each other and reflect the past and the future. Your South Node reflects your past, your karmic journeys, and where you come from. Any wisdom you have accumulated from your past lives is brought here in this world, armoring you for what lies ahead. On the other hand, your North Node reflects your future. It shows you your true destiny, your calling in this life. This concludes the basic table of your astrological chart and its representation.

After having completed that, it is time to dive even deeper to the planetary powers. What you will focus on is the 'detriment', the 'exaltation', and the 'fall.' These are the fundamental dignities of each planet. The detriment is the planet that is located exactly opposite to the sign it rules. In this case, the planet does not hold abundant strength over the specific sign. On the other hand, exaltation means that the specific sign does hold a strong position and impacts the planet. So, this means that the planet is most suitably positioned at that point. The planet's fall, of course, represents its least powerful position.

Sun rules Leo, but the sign opposite Leo is Aquarius. So the Sun is in detriment in the sign of Aquarius. Respectively, the Moon is in detriment in the sign of Capricorn. When it comes to Mercury, there is Sagittarius. Venus is in detriment in Scorpio, Mars in Libra, Jupiter in Gemini, Saturn in

Cancer, Uranus in Leo, Neptune in Virgo, and finally Pluto in Taurus.

Next step is for you to write down the exaltation and fall options of each planet in your chart. Sun is exalted in the sign of Aries and then falls in the sign of Libra. The Moon is exalted in Taurus and falls in Scorpio. Mercury is exalted in Virgo and falls in Pisces, whereas Venus is exalted in Pisces and falls in Virgo. Mars is exalted in Capricorn and falls in Cancer, while Jupiter is the exact opposite. Saturn is exalted in Libra and falls in Aries, Uranus is exalted in Scorpio and falls in Taurus. Neptune is exalted in Sagittarius and falls in Gemini and, lastly, Pluto is exalted in Leo and falls in Aquarius.

Another wonderful table that you should create (after all that!) is a table that features the elements, the modes, and trinities of the planets. This will also help you interpret your natal chart, which is awesome! As you know, there are four elements and each sign is characterized by a single element. Aries, Leo, and Sagittarius are in the element of fire. Taurus, Virgo, and Capricorn are in the element of earth. Gemini, Libra, and Aquarius are in the element of Air, while finally Cancer, Scorpio, and Pisces are in the element of water.

Regarding modes or modalities, Aries is cardinal, Leo is fixed, and Sagittarius is mutable. For earth signs, Taurus is fixed, Virgo is mutable, and Capricorn is cardinal. Next, Gemini is mutable, Libra is cardinal, and Aquarius is fixed. Lastly, in regards to the water signs, Cancer is cardinal, Scorpio is fixed, and Pisces is mutable. For the next phase, the trinities should be explained further. Aries is ruled by the first house and this is an angular house, representing action. The same goes for the tenth house, ruled by Capricorn, the seventh house ruled by Libra, and the fourth house ruled by Cancer.

In a similar pattern, we have Leo ruled by the fifth house,

which is a succedent house. This means that it is all about sustainment. The same happens with Taurus, ruled by the second house, Aquarius, ruled by the eleventh house and Scorpio, ruled by the eighth house. Cadent trinities are Sagittarius. ruled by the ninth house, Virgo, ruled by the sixth house, Gemini, ruled by the third house, and Pisces, ruled by the twelfth house.

In your natal chart, observe the outer wheel with the signs, and the inner wheel with the planets. When you lay out all the tables that you have prepared so far, you will be able to read your birth chart very accurately. If you are having difficulty in remembering how this works, think of an analogy that works for you. For example, the planets are the actors in a theatrical play, while the signs represent their characters, and the houses compose the actual scene on which the actors perform.

A Brief Guide to Astrological Houses and Signs

The first house is about who you are, and it is ruled by Aries, since the ruling planet is Mars. It is relevant to the way you look and aligns with your physical appearance. Everyone notices it, so it is what we project to the world! It is also a reflection of your childhood experiences. How did you grow up and how did you start interacting with others in the world? All that non-verbal communication is reflected in the first house, and essentially this is the place of your higher self. Moving on to the second house, this is ruled by Taurus and its ruling planet is Venus. It is all about creating! You are building a life for yourself, and therefore Taurus is associated with how you feel about *you*. It depicts your self-esteem and confidence, your self-worth and moral code.

Gemini is the sign of the third house, ruled by Mercury, and it refers to communication on all levels. This house is associated with your siblings, friends, and family, as well as any other person you interact with in your life. It refers to your everyday life and defines how you behave on several occasions. Apart from that, it is the house of intellect, and offers you the chance to adapt to various situations. Corresponding with the energy of Cancer, the fourth house is ruled by Uranus and symbolizes family, along with intimate relationships.

The fifth house is ruled by Leo and the Sun, allowing you to show your creativity to the world! It shows your personal style and how you explore your uniqueness. Your sense of romance and love is also determined by the fifth house, while your relationships with children and how you get along with them is another aspect affected by this particular house. Next is the sixth house, and this is ruled by Virgo. This house corresponds to the energy of Mercury, even though some claim that it is Chiron that rules it. Health and wellness are influenced by this house.

Libra rules the seventh house, corresponding to the energy of Venus. This house is quite special, as it offers you a glimpse at your direct relationships. Are you leaning towards others or are you running away from them? How do you cope with intimacy and feeling close to other people? Is this something that you enjoy, or is it something that you dread? You can see that it is the exact opposite of the first house, which is pretty interesting! Moving on to the eighth house, this is often referred to as the 'haunted house.' It might sound intimidating, but this house relates to sex, death, and the occult, as well as changes of all sorts. As you may have guessed, the eighth house is ruled by Pluto and Scorpio.

The ninth house is ruled by Jupiter and Sagittarius. It has to do with exploration and a constant eagerness to find out more about the world. You may engage in philosophical quests through this house and you may find yourself in an attempt to discover what lies beyond your grasp. You become curious, wiser, and you feel a deep need to travel, to indulge in new experiences. On the other hand, the tenth house is ruled by Capricorn and Saturn. It lies opposite to Cancer, representing a fatherly figure. This house governs your image and the way you appear to others around you. It signifies your success and drives your ambitions.

Before reaching the end, the eleventh house is ruled by Aquarius and Uranus. Linked to your humanitarian pursuits, this is also the house that deals with karmic relationships and alliances that are formed in life. You will also see that it is closely associated with revolutionary concepts and ideas. Finally, the twelfth house is ruled by the energy of Pisces and Neptune. People often call this the "unseen house." This house has to do with things that you cannot see, yet you can feel and understand. It is about the unconscious and escapism. Consequently, this is the house linked to spirituality and intuition.

As soon as you fully comprehend the exact patterns in which every sign and planet collaborate with each other, you become more aware of how the universe affects your very existence. The houses are there to show you how each different energy is manifesting on the earth, influencing you and everyone else around you. This is a magical process that unfolds before your eyes, through the power of these celestial objects shining bright and sharing their precious energy with you!

7

BUILDING THE TOWERING ARCHITECTURE THAT IS YOUR DREAM LIFE: MOON LIFE PLANNING MASTERY

Up to this point, you have gained great insights on how the Moon affects your life on so many different levels. Now is the time to start planning your life based on the full moon and the various moon phases! This is how you are going to construct the masterpiece of your existence, exactly the way you have been dreaming of. I know you are excited about it and you cannot wait for all those marvelous things lying ahead! So, let's focus on the more practical side of Moon interpretation.

As the Moon revolves around the Earth, it influences our planet significantly. Of course, this influence is not the same during the lunar cycle. As I have pointed out earlier in this book, there are many factors taking a toll on the Moon's influence. This is why it is of the essence to truly comprehend when is the time to sit still and recover, as well as when is the perfect time to set your intentions and watch them turn into reality.

I hope that you have been paying attention so far, because the Moon has got so much to offer! Indeed, it is fascinating to see the great impact the Moon can have in your life. It is especially important to know when to focus on actions and when to lay back and remain idle if you are going to make the most out of your lunar experience. So choose your battles wisely!

At the beginning of the lunar cycle, you have no energy. You need to recover and regain your strength in order to pursue your goals a little later. So this is not the time to claim what is rightfully yours, as you will be laboring with no result, and your efforts will be in vain. However, you can always ponder and dream about what you wish to manifest! Slowly, you will be able to start making plans and setting your intentions. Just before the first quarter of the Moon, you will see that your energy is gradually piling up.

Upon entering the waxing gibbous, you have begun to regain your powers and now it is time to take action. What can you do to ensure that your intentions do not go unnoticed? How can you make use of your powers, in order to refine and nurture those goals? This is a greatly beneficial period that can actually influence your life through the energy of the Moon. You are driven by a higher power, an eternal force flowing within you. Have faith in the process and trust the Moon to receive what you want in life.

With the full moon, you should be celebrating. reflecting on what you have wished to receive. The Sun and the Moon have aligned fully, allowing you to praise their magnitude and appreciate the wonders of nature. Prepare yourself to receive gracefully, giving thanks to the universe for everything that you have already received in your life. Feel the mystical aura of the full moon surrounding you, feeling complete and accomplished.

The waning gibbous moon phase is perfect to receive and be grateful. Share those blessings with the world, staying true to your higher self. Find your calling in life and stick with it, before reflecting as the third quarter phase arrives. If your intentions have not been transformed into reality, think about it. What has gone wrong? What could you have done differently? Learn from your experiences and get ready to try again in a little while. For now, in the waning crescent phase, you are encouraged to take it down a notch. Rest, release all the tension that has accumulated thus far, and sigh with relief.

You have made it to the end of yet another lunar cycle. Enjoy stillness, take a deep breath, and let's begin one more cycle around the Earth! A timeless journey that affects us all deserves to be celebrated every single time, because every cycle is unique and holds so many wonderful treasures within! Just reach out and be open to receive them.

A LOOK AT THE DAILY MOON

Every single lunar cycle represents a full journey towards growth. By taking a look at the daily Moon, you can align your life in a way that makes the most out of this powerful celestial element! However, you must first understand how each lunar cycle works. From what you saw earlier, there is a time to sit still and rest in the new moon. Then, there is a time to set intentions and take actions. Right after that, the time comes when you celebrate and be open to receive your blessings. There is a time to reflect and possibly identify any wrongdoings or obstacles standing in the way.

Another factor that you should take into consideration when interpreting the Moon cycle is the zodiac sign on which the Moon falls. This special detail allows you to fully align with the universe and promote your personal growth in the world. According to the specific zodiac sign that affects each lunar cycle, you can adjust your life and ensure that you maximize your odds of achieving your goals, ultimately reaching success. Feel free to explore the lunar cycles of each zodiac sign and understand how they influence you personally.

Aries drives your will to succeed and therefore sparks your passion. During the new moon, Aries allows you to start fresh and identify any challenges that may come along the way. In the waxing moon, this is the sign that drives you to push forward, and keeps motivating you throughout the lunar cycle. During the full moon, it is time for you to take charge of your life and Aries will make sure you do! As the waning moon arrives, Aries will enable you to reclaim your power and adjust your course to make the most of your efforts.

On the other hand, Taurus offers you the opportunity to slow down a little! In the new moon, you will be motivated to appreciate the present and its pleasurable moments. Even if you have not been mindful of your blessings, Taurus will help you. In the waxing moon, Taurus will see that you lay strong foundations for the life you deserve and anticipate. The full moon is the perfect time to celebrate your accomplishments and take the action required to achieve your goals. Abundance and gratitude are prevalent during the waning moon.

Gemini is outgoing and adventurous as a sign. If you are eager to communicate with the universe, then this is a great time to do so... especially during the new moon! In the waxing moon, you prepare yourself for whatever it takes in order to realize your dreams and manifestations. During the full moon, you will be able to ask questions and seek the answers that will assist in your goal-setting. Finally, as the Moon enters the waning period, you will be encouraged to evaluate your course so far.

The sign of Cancer is emotional and vulnerable, focusing on your inner self. In the new moon, Cancer invites you to introspect and identify any emotional issues that have been holding you back from achieving your goals. During the waxing period of the lunar cycle, you should modify your actions as per the realization of your emotional triggers. The full moon is a great time for you to embrace your emotional vulnerability, rather than shying away from emotions altogether! Lastly, you will see how these emotions actually affect you in the waning moon.

You already know that Leo is daring and brave! In the new moon, Leo will urge you to face your fears and reflect on their meaning. During the waxing period, you will be asked to conquer those fears. You should realize why they have such an effect on you before you can take action and crush them. Under the full moon, Leo will guide you towards seeing your truth and letting go of your hesitations. In the waning period, you will be ready to take pleasure from your life as it is and boost your confidence!

Moving on to the sign of Virgo: This is definitely the time to organize things and keep them neat and tidy. In the new moon, you will be driven to form new habits that benefit you in the long run. Your mind will shift in a positive way that allows you to be happy and accomplish your goals. During the waxing moon, you must focus on understanding whether or not your routines are good for you. In the full moon, Virgo will enable you to reflect on your current situation and see if this is what truly makes you happy. Finally, the waning period brings clarity in your life and offers you a glimpse at the wider picture.

Libra is the sign of balance and alignment. The new moon in Libra offers you a chance to understand if something has fallen out of balance. If so, what can you do to remedy the situation? Even if you can't do that just yet, you should try to let your displeasure go. It may be time to change your perspective and this is what the waxing period allows you to do! In the full moon, you fully comprehend what messes with your alignment and you prepare yourself to let go. As the Moon continues its course and you enter the waning period, you should listen to your heart and let it take the lead.

Mystery and change define Scorpio, which is the sign that allows you to take a good look deep within you. In the full moon, set your intentions to truly understand who you are and what you enjoy. Understand your passions and deepest desires, so that you start pursuing them during the waxing moon. As the full moon approaches, it is time to set out on your path towards bringing those passions and desires into your life. Finally, the waning period is the time for you to interpret your behavior and see why you do things the way you do.

If you wish to flourish, Sagittarius will lead the way. The new moon in Sagittarius enables you to step forward and claim the life that you deserve! Discover what makes your heart beat faster and set the intentions of receiving those blessings. In the waxing moon, you should identify the obstacles that hinder your happiness and make sure you take action. The full moon is the time to focus on your truth, releasing any negativity and past experiences that have dragged you down. Last but not least, the waning period is when you come to terms with your emotional self.

Unlike Sagittarius, Capricorn will bring you back to Earth. In the new moon, you will be motivated to set more realistic intentions that are aligned with yourself. What is your true calling and what do you need to succeed in your life's purpose? The waxing moon is the time to make necessary changes, in order to accomplish your goals. Get real in the full moon, with Capricorn awakening you and pushing you towards self-realization. Be efficient and see those goals turn into reality during the waning period.

Focus on you and you alone when the new moon is in Aquarius. A free spirit, Aquarius guides you to discover who you really are. Choose to be independent and work towards self-accomplishment throughout the waxing period of the moon. Under the full moon, you can communicate with your deepest self and bring to surface your desires. Express yourself, do not hold back, and do not postpone getting what you want. In the waning period, this is exactly what you should focus on!

Wrapping up the zodiac signs, Pisces is all about ethereal spirituality. In the new moon, set your intentions regarding your spiritual self and focus on your transformation. During the waxing period, you will be able to explore your strengths and weaknesses, becoming wiser in the process. The full moon brings awareness to your emotional state and allows you to see why you really feel that way. Finally, the waning period lets all the sunshine in and brings clarity into your soul, as you truly see who you are meant to be in this life!

How to Start a Moon Journal for Personal Growth

Visual representations are always great assets when it comes to focusing on different aspects of your existence and your connection to the world. This is why it is so crucial to keep a moon journal, as you can truly delve into the mysteries of lunar cycles and explore their effects on your life. Are you looking forward to transforming your existence and welcoming enlightenment? Then you need a pen or pencil, colorful markers, a cute journal that speaks into your soul, and, of course, a positive attitude!

What you need to do first is to draw the lunar cycle in as much detail as possible. You can find templates online, so you can print them out and glue them into your journal. The printables should show you the moon phases (new moon, waxing moon, full moon, waning moon etc.) and have them as a reference. They all form a cycle, starting with stillness, moving all the way into action, and then flowing down again. In this way, through this visualization, you will realize how the energy flows, and how all these phases are interconnected.

With every lunar cycle, you should concentrate on setting new intentions. Once again, you can plan ahead based on the zodiac sign where the Moon falls every month. For instance, if you wish to set spiritual intentions, then Pisces Moon is the perfect time to do that! Use your creativity in your journal for each particular lunar cycle. You can draw pictures or print them online, or even use old scrapbooks and magazines. Whatever makes you feel happy and works for you is great here, as you create this themed cycle with the moon phases for yourself only. Give that cycle a name and then create a diary.

It is equally important to keep a journal of your actions throughout the specific lunar cycle. You can turn the page and make room for a detailed monthly diary, where each day you add everything you have done towards realizing your goals. This will be your monthly challenge! Again, draw and fill it out in a way that motivates you to come back to the journal. In this diary, you can also add how you feel and describe your mood. As a result, you may see what effects the Moon has on you! It will help you better understand yourself.

It is also advised that you keep a special weekly spread with your actions and anything else you wish to reflect on more carefully. On a different page you can focus on each moon phase and analyze what this is all about. In the new moon, you will concentrate on setting your new intentions, while in the waxing period you will take action. Write down your specific objectives for this exact week and monitor your progress. This is going to be tangible proof of whether or not you have accomplished your goals. Furthermore, tracking what happens in your life can serve as a way to identify the barriers that have prevented you from reaching your goals.

Be consistent with your moon journal and you will be able to fully comprehend yourself, shedding light to those parts that you have not even realized are there! By tracking your mood, your actions, and the boundaries that keep you from enjoying what you want, you will have the opportunity to modify your behavior and reach happiness! If you are determined to achieve personal growth and use the eternal power of the Moon to guide you in your path, then you should make a habit of creating a moon journal and staying true to it. After a few lunar cycles, its impact is going to be astonishing!

8

BATHE IN THE MOON'S ENERGY TO CLEANSE WHAT NO LONGER SERVES YOU

The Moon is magical, offering its healing properties to you. Immerse yourself in its powerful energy and get in full alignment with the universe. Once you start living in harmony with nature and its mysteries, you will see that everything comes together. Build a strong bond and heal yourself, letting go of whatever no longer serves your life purpose.

Even if you have been hurt before, the new moon represents new beginnings. Start fresh and delve into the Moon's power. This is another motivation for you to pursue happiness, self-accomplishment, and success through your actions. Plant the seeds that you wish to grow in your garden, wishing on the Moon for prosperity and successful outcomes. It is a time of rebirth, rejuvenation, and absolute dedication to your cause! Do not let anything poison your soul, keeping you away from what you can achieve in life.

There are many ways for you to embrace and harness the lunar energy. Bathe under the moonlight to feel its power flowing right through you. Light a candle and reflect on the moon phases, feeling what they represent every single night. Gaze up at the sky, observing the Moon and its exact position. The Moon is able to see your soul, so feel free to open up and receive its blessings! Visualize your goals and feel totally relaxed, trusting in the Moon for accomplishing them in the end. Even if it takes a while, the entire experience is worth it!

Connect yourself to the Moon, creating an everlasting bond that is hard to break. Embrace your spirituality and allow the Moon to guide you. Your inner child is trapped in isolation, and through this powerful connection you can let go of past traumas, enabling your inner child to finally breathe and become liberated. The Moon represents your feminine divine energy, your intuition, and your psychic abilities. Therefore, being connected to it means that you accept your spiritual self and achieve a holistic balance in your life.

The Moon is so powerful and it cleanses all negativity from your life! If you allow it to flow through you, the Moon will get rid of anything toxic and help you elevate your vibrational frequencies. It will assist you on your path towards healing your deeper self. No matter how painful the process might be, in the end you are going to be reborn. You will be stronger than ever, more confident in your own powers, and fully aligned with the universe.

HEALING YOURSELF WITH THE ENERGY OF THE MOON

Your body is your temple, and you must think of it as a sacred vessel. Many people forget just how important it is to keep their body in a pristine state, seeking health and rejecting anything that might hinder their progress. Be in tune with the lunar cycle, modifying your actions accordingly to reach the highest levels of spiritual awareness. Learn when is the time to rest, recover, heal, and introspect. Then, get ready to fuel your passion, take necessary action, and nurture your goals, ensuring that you meet them by the end of the cycle.

During the waning period, as the Moon goes into darkness, you should take a break to focus on your health. This is the time to relax, clearing your chakras and cleansing your aura. Get rid of toxicity in your life, sigh with relief, and engage in meditation for optimal results in communicating with your inner self. Deep breathing will help you dispose of anxiety and in turn, listen to what your body is telling you. Be conscious and set your intentions mindfully. In the waxing period, you should focus on energizing your body, taking the steps required to reach your goals. Let the positive energy of the Moon flow right through you, elevating your frequency, and therefore welcoming all those glorious intentions into your reality.

Below you will find a full moon ritual that can help you heal with the power of the Moon! Use that to concentrate on positive vibes and let go of the barriers that mess with your balance. Furthermore, it is beneficial to take moon baths by observing the Moon during the lunar cycle, and letting its glow shine through you. Be open to receiving its energy, welcoming it into your life, and feeling the Moon as it blesses you with its special powers! Engage in power charged meditations that enable you to delve deeper and align with the cosmos. The world is your oyster if you simply understand how it works!

During the full moon, a great way to supercharge your life is to dance under the moonlight! Let go of your worries and feel like a child again! This is your time to enjoy, relish those moments of innocence and dance exactly the way you feel like it. No one is there to judge you or make you feel uncomfortable. So start swaying and dancing to the beat of your favorite music or simply follow your inner rhythm. It is a therapeutic method to release negative energy and let go of your emotional baggage. On the other hand, you should understand your limitations during this point of the lunar cycle. Do not make any sudden decisions based on an impulse, as the full moon tends to heighten all emotions and create more drama. Instead, take some time to distance yourself from any situation and relax.

Embrace harmony from within, listening to your body throughout each lunar cycle. Feel its positive effects on you both physically and mentally. This is an ongoing journey towards self-growth and expansion! You should always be grateful for what you have already received in your life, praising the universe for the abundance you enjoy. Allow your body to heal naturally, without putting any pressure on it. Instead, cleanse your chakras to create a channel connecting you to the Earth and the sky above. Receive the nurturing properties of the Moon and watch the magic unfold.

Leave Space for Miracles to Happen

Everything in life happens for a reason. As we are part of the universe, we are divine! Therefore, we are responsible for all the blessings that we receive. All the miracles that we seek in the world are essentially our making. It is up to us to see the silver lining in every single misstep or difficult experience. Even in the darkest of times, we should learn valuable lessons from those negative things that happen. We must accept them and forgive them. Only in this way can we remain calm and let go of the negativity, so that the true miracles can eventually brighten our life. And this cannot happen without cleansing and creating the space for those miracles.

You should take the initiative and cleanse your life of everything bad that has been holding you back! I am going to show you how to get rid of those toxic thoughts and harmful patterns in your life, how to release the lower energies and make room for high frequencies. The full moon is the perfect timing for you to forgive and heal, as this is when your emotions are heightened and you become most spiritually aware. You should therefore carry out a full moon ritual to cleanse from everything negative, and make space for all the wonderful things that you are about to receive.

First of all, create a sacred space. I have referred to this earlier in the book. Cleanse the atmosphere from negative auras and invite new, positive auras instead in a place you feel safe. You can burn sage for a thorough cleansing of the atmosphere, Palo Santo sticks, or even scented candles and incense. Then, start writing down on a piece of paper all the things you wish to let go of. You can write a list, always beginning with the words, *I release...* and then continue on to name everything you wish to release. This is spiritual purging for you, so you can expect being emotional throughout the ritual.

Be gentle, in order to be the best version of your life. As you are writing down your list, you will realize that you feel like a huge burden has been lifted off your chest. Gradually, you will start feeling happier and this means that you no longer hold any grudges, or any anger towards those things you release. At the end of the list, you should conclude with the following statement: *I demand that all bodies, thoughts, vibrations, frequencies, and patterns that are anchoring the energy I wish to release, actually leave me and my energy. I demand that they leave me on all layers of existence, beyond dimensions and time. You do not belong here with me. I declare that this is the truth, according to my highest self and the greatest good.*

Be present in the moment and read through your list out loud, concluding with your statement. After doing that, it is now time to burn the paper! Use a tray or a pot to avoid any accidents. Pick up a candle or a lighter and burn the paper, as the physical representation of this release. Watch the paper burn and feel the beneficial effects of this ritual within your soul. Pick up the ashes and dispose of them safely. Take a deep breath and sigh with relief. By completing this ritual, you have made it clear that you are open to receive the miracles you are looking forward to. So, now it is up to the universe to grant you what you have requested!

9

THE NEXT LEVEL: MOON MAGIC MASTERY

I am positive that you are already feeling the magnitude of the Moon energy in your life. It is a thrilling experience and I could not be happier for you! Now it is time to learn how to master Moon magic and optimize your success in every single lunar cycle. Once you understand how to harness the energy of the Moon, you will be blessed with an eternal gift of fully aligning with nature, and can receive its blessings without anything holding you back.

One of the biggest steps for you to take towards utilizing the celestial elements to your advantage is to create a spiritual altar. I know that it might sound impossible to have a dedicated place to call your own, without anyone touching it. Especially if you live with a bunch of other people. When part of a large family, for example, privacy tends to be underrated or even ignored completely. However, this is crucial to your future as a glorious witch that wants to conquer nature through spells, rituals, meditation, and so much more.

If you are having trouble deciding where to place your altar, then you need to close your eyes and understand where it feels right. It can be in your bedroom, in the backyard, in the living room, or anywhere else. Moreover, it doesn't matter how much space it takes! You are free to decide, as long as it makes you feel comfortable and safe. In order to enhance safety, you should include a white and a red candle in your altar. Black salt in a cute little jar is also great, as well as pyrite crystal. It is important that you light your candles on a daily basis, or at least when you meditate.

From that point, you can use your imagination to add some character in your altar. Other crystals and incense, scented candles and flowers, plants and small decorative statuettes, your journal or other books that inspire you, can all be used to maximize the spiritual power of your altar. You can also include pictures of your loved ones or your ancestors, as they are guiding your spirit. If you practice tarot readings, then keep the tarot oracle cards close by, along with a comfortable cushion. Anything that makes you feel at home is great to add in your personal sacred place.

When you are at your altar, nothing can harm you! The time you spend there is absolutely magical, so make sure that you nurture this feeling of safety and protection. Practice your spells and rituals, meditate and engage in deep breathing exercises, write in your journal, and of course indulge in chakra cleansing. You can also manifest what you wish to receive in life, express your gratitude, and perform any ritual you believe helps you in your spiritual path.

MEDITATIONS AND RITUALS FOR THE FULL MOON

The full moon can feel so electric, since all energies are on high alert. As a result, magic is most potent during this time of the lunar cycle. Those 72 hours around the full moon are the best for you to practice any full moon ritual or meditation, maximizing their effectiveness. It is entirely up to you how you are going to take advantage of these magnificent hours when the full moon illuminates you in its healing powers.

There are many different things that you can do during the full moon. It doesn't have to be anything fancy. You can simply gather your crystals and go outside on your porch (or maybe by the beach), basking under the full moon and bathing in its glorious healing light. Give thanks to the full moon and connect on a deeper level, honoring its very core. Show your loving gratitude to the Moon for every single blessing that has come into your life. This is a great and simple, yet extremely powerful, way to express your appreciation.

If you are determined to conduct a full moon ritual, you must first check the zodiac sign to see which astrological sign the Moon is under. After identifying the exact properties of the specific full moon, you will be able to adjust your ritual for optimal results. In this way, you will be working with the particular energies surrounding the atmosphere instead of deciding on impulse what to manifest. That being said, you can still manifest whatever you want! A tarot reading is another wonderful asset in your hands, so you can call in any deities you feel might enhance your ritual.

Prior to the ritual itself, you should focus on meditation. Take deep breaths and listen to some relaxing music which inspires you and allows you to transcend into the universe. Concentrate and be present in the moment, while casting a circle and creating the sacred space for you to proceed with your ritual. You can use any scented candles, add your crystals, and use any other item that you think will help you meditate. As you are grounding yourself, you also need to be aware of the specific elements you are going to bring into the ritual. If the Moon falls under a water sign, then water should be prevalent during the ritual.

The witching hour is ideal for you to perform your ritual. This is of course around midnight, when the energy is at its peak! What you need to do is define what your heart truly desires and manifest it under the full moon. The secret lies within asking with a pure heart. Visualize the energy of the Moon beaming down on you. Then, imagine that you are holding that pure silvery light into your palms and you are channeling it into whatever you wish to manifest.

A wonderful way for you to shower yourself with the energy of the Moon is to purify your sacral chakra and channel the moonlight through that, causing your entire body to be overwhelmed by this magnificent beam of light. Keep in mind that magic is your innate nature, so this should come naturally to you. Be mindful of the spells you are casting and the energy that you are releasing. According to what you wish to achieve, it would be advisable not to perform those rituals exactly on the full moon. On the contrary, you may find it more beneficial to conduct these rituals and cleansing procedures a day earlier or later than the full moon.

When there are eclipses taking place during a specific lunar cycle, you are especially advised to wait it out and perform your rituals later. Otherwise, you would be risking that energy backfiring on you. After all, nature might interpret your rituals as a means of manipulation and this is never a good thing. Even if you have the nicest intentions, you must be patient and enjoy the full moon without manifesting anything on that particular night. The energy will be high even on the next night for you to benefit from through your rituals.

Insights on Different Moons & Eclipses

There are several terms that might baffle you when trying to interpret the lunar cycle. I am going to explain some of these terms, so that you can fully comprehend what they mean, and understand the universe even more profoundly. First of all, I am sure you have heard that Mercury is in retrograde, and that this can affect people on many levels. The truth is that Mercury does not change its course and does not move backwards. However, it appears to do so!

The reason behind this phenomenon is the distance between Mercury and the Sun. Since this is in fact the closest planet when it comes to the Sun, its orbit is much smaller. As a result, it seems that at a specific point it slows down a little and the Earth is able to pass by. This is when it appears to be moving in retrograde. Although this is an illusion, you still need to remember that this phenomenon brings turbulence to the cosmos. So do not make any final decisions and do not choose to do anything radical then.

Eclipses happen when the Sun, the Moon, and the Earth align with each other. A total eclipse of the Moon is called a "Red Moon" or a "Blood Moon." This happens when the Moon travels through the Earth's 'umbra', which is basically the center of its shadow. As a result, the Sun does not illuminate the Moon directly. On the contrary, the light is reflected on the Earth and then illuminates the Moon. So the Moon appears to be a reddish color, although sometimes the color can range from orange to dark yellow.

This can be an emotionally challenging time, with the Red Moon affecting people's sleep patterns and overall mood. As mentioned above, the umbra is the inner part of a shadow. The Earth's umbra causes the lunar eclipses, which can either be partial or full. 'Penumbra', on the other hand, is the lighter part of the shadow. Finally, there is also the 'antumbra.' This is the external rim of the shadow that is visible beyond the umbra. It is especially evident during the annular eclipse, which takes place when the Moon's surface covers the Sun entirely, creating a fiery ring all around.

Moving on to the "Blue Moon", this is yet another spectacular phenomenon up in the sky! Although there are several occasions when the Moon does appear blue, in fact a Blue Moon simply means the second full moon within a single calendar month. It is a rather rare phenomenon, taking place approximately every 30 months! If you are wondering why, then you should take into account that a lunar cycle lasts around 29.5 days. However, months have 30 or 31 days. So, this leaves room for the Blue Moon to occur.

If you are interested in learning what a "Flower Moon" is, you will be happy to know that it is the full moon in May, which is compared to a flower that slowly blooms in spring. In January, we have the "Wolf Moon." February is the time for the "Snow Moon", March is when the "Worm Moon" occurs, and April is great for the "Pink Moon." After May, in June we have the "Strawberry Moon", and then July is when the "Buck Moon" occurs. A "Sturgeon Moon" is in August, "Harvest Moon" in September or October, divided into a full "Corn Moon" or "Hunter's Moon." To complete the monthly full moon calendar, November is the "Beaver Moon" and December is the "Cold Moon."

10

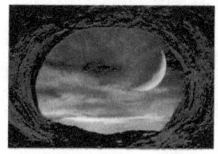

POWER CHARGED MOON CYCLE AND NEW MOON ASTROLOGY GUIDED MEDITATIONS

There is no better time in the lunar cycle than the new moon for you to manifest what you wish to receive in life. As a result, you should make sure that you supercharge your spirituality and establish a deep connection with the Moon, as one more lunar cycle begins. This is a key element if you want to take advantage of the glorious power of the Moon towards projecting your dreams and desires into reality.

Once again, you can always combine these meditations with tarot readings! Depending on the exact phase of the Moon, your readings can enlighten you on so many different things. For instance, the new moon is a great time to use your tarot oracle readings for new things, while the waxing moon period is perfect for things you already have in your life. The full moon is all about Intuition, whereas the waning period is ideal for eliminating things from your life. Work around these moon phases and watch these mysteries unfold before your eyes!

Below I have gathered some of the most effective, powerful, magical meditations for you to try out during the new moon. As you can see, they focus on different aspects of the very same thing. This is the time for new beginnings, the time to let go of the past and move forward. Set new intentions, take action to bring them into your life, and become aware of the blockages that hinder your progress. Heal, recover, rise from the ashes, and claim what is rightfully yours, always with the help of the omnipresent Moon.

GUIDED MEDITATION TO MANIFEST YOUR DREAMS

What would you like to bring into your life? Through this guided meditation, you will be able to manifest all those marvelous things, and enjoy the benefits of the new moon towards supercharging your new intentions.

For this meditation, sit somewhere comfortably. Find your spiritual altar and place your palms on your lap. Close your eyes and focus on your breathing. As you are breathing in through your nose, feel your lungs filling with fresh air. Breathe out through your mouth, emptying your lungs until you feel your belly button lift. Repeat the same pattern of deep breaths in order for your body to relax and become lighter.

Visualize just one thing that you would like to welcome into your life. Focus on this thought, trying to analyze why you want that. Why of all things have you chosen to bring this into your life? What will it offer you? How will it affect your everyday life and what impact will it have on your spiritual journey? What kind of feelings will it spark? You do not need to think of the way you are going to bring this into your life, as you must have faith in the process. Feel those emotions of positivity, pleasure, love, security, everything that is associated with bringing this specific thing into your life.

Repeat to yourself: *I manifest what is best for the good of all.*

Keep your eyes closed. You can repeat this as many times as you like so that you become absolutely certain that you are going to actually acquire it at the end of this cycle. When you are ready to regain full consciousness, do so without letting go of your certainty. Whatever it is you have manifested will indeed flourish and be brought into your reality. You trust the process and have no doubts about it. What you have manifested is already yours!

Now let go, allowing the universe to work its magic. Remember to take deep breaths. Breathe in through your nose. Open your mouth and let all the air out completely. Repeat the same process twice again, so as to release any tension that has piled up. Feel utterly relaxed, as you begin to stretch your hands above your head. Press your palms together right above your head, and then move them down until you reach your heart and chest.

Remember, *what you think you become, what you feel you attract, what you imagine you create*, and be grateful for the experience. Give thanks to the universe for granting your desires and manifesting that special thing you have attracted into your life. I am sure that by now a huge smile has lit up your face! You feel that sense of accomplishment overwhelming you! It is that exceptional feeling of fullness you are experiencing. Take a few moments to enjoy this feeling and then get on with your day, always keeping in mind the magnificent experience you had.

GUIDED MEDITATION TO CLEAR FINANCIAL BLOCKS & ATTRACT MONEY

Who doesn't want some extra money, especially if it is completely out of the blue? Through this guided meditation, you will get the chance to clear any negativity that results in financial blocks, making room for more money coming your way!

Close your eyes and relax, relaxing your body. Breathe in and out deeply, slowly, focusing on nothing but your breath. Feel safe in the present moment. Release the tension and pressure in every single muscle of your body, letting go of all burdens. With every breath, you relax even more and you delve deeper into your creative mind. Now travel away, visualizing that you are in a verdant forest with the Sun rays shining down on you gracefully.

As the Sun showers you with its golden light, repeat: *I am worthy of financial abundance and love. I am richly rewarded for everything I give to the world. I am fully supported, protected, and deeply loved. Prosperity comes into my life effortlessly. Money is good and I know that. Money is easy and it flows to me with great ease. I feel such a deep sense of peace.* Through the Law of Attraction, everything you want comes easily to you.

Soak in this wonderful experience, observing the peaceful landscape and noticing even the slightest detail. Listen to the leaves gently flowing with the autumn breeze, while smelling the delightful aromas of nature. Think, *I am in alignment with the source of all creation. Everything I need is already here for me. My life is perfectly synchronized. I am in tune with my higher self and the world around me. The universe is taking care of everything I need.* As you are observing closer, you allow yourself to be enveloped in pure luxury.

Continue your positive affirmations, so that you visualize those marvelous images and clear your sacral chakra. Think, *I attract great and wonderful experiences. I bathe in unpretentious prosperity. I deserve the best and I accept it now with open arms. Furthermore, I receive with ease everything I want in my life, all that my heart desires.* Slowly, the Sun goes down to sleep and the Moon takes its place with its healing silvery light. Remember to be thankful: *Thank you for my endless abundance, thank you universe for my wealth. Thank you for bringing me unlimited money. I have planted the seed in my subconscious mind and now I am already reaping the fruit of my manifestations.*

Finally, feel gratitude overwhelming you for all that you have received so far. All this money, all this abundance in your life is brought to you by the universe: *I am filled with gratitude and aligned with the universe, allowing this energy constantly coming my way and bringing me wealth beyond limits. Thank you.* When you are done, slowly open your eyes and feel that lovely sense of abundance flowing through you. You are fully aware of what the universe has granted you, so you feel at peace with the world and enjoy life to its fullest potential!

GUIDED MEDITATION FOR INNER HEALING

Do you wish to prepare yourself for something new in your life? Do you feel wounded by the past? This guided meditation will allow you to let go of the past, heal your inner self, and recharge your spiritual energy, getting ready for a glorious future ahead.

Tend to your spiritual altar and sit comfortably, closing your eyes and concentrating on deep breathing. Let your breath flow easily, effortlessly, like a summer breeze gently rocking the boats at the seashore. Clear your mind and open your heart to receive the light energy that is all around you. Visualize the sky with millions of stars scattered all around and shining down on you eternally. Imagine the new moon that you cannot see, but you can feel through its energy that connects you to the entire universe.

Receive the healing properties of the new moon, as you are blessed by its powerful energy. The new moon is the perfect time to set intentions and create visions. It is also great for clearing your path, letting go of the negativity, and focusing solely on positive new beginnings. What do you wish to create in this new lunar cycle? Bring that into your mind and clear your thoughts. What do you want to receive? What are your goals? Set your intentions deep inside your heart. Watch them grow as the Moon becomes lighter and shines even more beautifully.

Everything that surrounds you contributes to the success of your goals, allowing you to bring them into reality. Imagine how everything supports you in your direction towards fulfilling your goals. Continue looking up in the sky, observing its vastness. Breathe in and out deeply, feeling the new chapter in your life that has already begun. You have turned over a new leaf and the universe supports you fully, unconditionally. Nothing can harm you, as long as you have that vast power by your side! You are refreshed, ready to take on the new challenges in your life.

Your life is moving in the direction of your desire and everything is fully aligned to help you reach your goals. You will grow side by side with the new moon, expanding with each phase, and glowing with the full moon. As the new moon shines brighter every day of the lunar cycle, you will also radiate with light and joy! There is nothing able to bring you down, since you have the support of the divine. You have been blessed with the energy of the new moon and nothing can hinder your progress on this spiritual path you have set out to walk on.

As you have let go of all the toxicity, release yourself from unwanted and harmful habits, as you are now reborn. Breathe deeply and feel the energy of the Moon guiding you in your course. You are not alone. You are healed and you are ready to start afresh. Stay in this feeling for as long as you like. Then open your eyes gently and sigh with relief.

GUIDED MEDITATION WITH THE ANGELS TO BRING ETHERIC ENERGY INTO YOUR LIFE

The angels are powerful beings that can help you replenish your depleted energy and reach the highest levels of vibrational frequencies. Through this guided meditation, you join the wonderful energy of the angels, and become blessed to manifest your fullest potential.

Archangel Michael, Uriel, Gabriel, and Raphael are by your side, connecting with you during this meditation. Create your sacred space and allow the pillars of light from above to wash down on you. Let go of any attachments, body aches, worries. And just for now, let go of attachments to anyone else in your life, and whatever else you have to do today. Let go of the mental body and your thoughts. Tune in to the pure love glowing within you, flowing through you. This is your truth emerging from within you. It is recalibrating you, so that you become open to receive the blessings of divine light into your life.

Channel this light all the way above your head, creating a strong bond and a deep connection between your body and the cosmos above. Communicate with the archangels, as you open yourself and get ready to receive the light transmission to illuminate your consciousness. This is revealing your direct unity with all that is, while also maintaining your individuality. Moving downwards, this golden light is channeled from your crown chakra to your mind and brings heightened awareness and clarity.

Traveling even further down to your throat, this glorious light allows you to speak clearly and purifies this center of energy. Next is your heart, with the light shining brightly and warming it up. Your heart opens and is ready to receive the golden light frequency of awakened solar love, cleansed of all worry and fear. This love allows consciousness to expand and clears your etheric energy, empowering you to shine brighter and vibrate at higher levels.

Allow the same wondrous light to travel even further below to your willpower center, enabling you to act based on your inspiration, in alignment with divine love. Feel empowered and recharged, able to manifest blessings you wish to receive in your life. Now move towards your sacral chakra, purifying this creative center, empowering your truest divine embodiment to anchor down and embody your etheric energy. This will allow your body to remain grounded, blessed by eternal love. Feel that you are safe, supported, and empowered to embody the highest form of love.

Now that your body is purified, your heart is open, you are ready to receive love in its purest form and all the endless possibilities will flow through you. You are blessed by the universe, guided by the archangels. A new beginning is here, now. Reach out and seize the day, opening up to new experiences that help you continue on your spiritual path. Feel the energy surrounding you. You have been blessed and you have received abundance in your life, through the etheric energy of the celestial beings shining down on you. Open your eyes, feel that sensation of completeness, and give thanks to the universe for being so generous.

11

THE LUNAR MASTERY 30-MINUTE DAILY RITUAL TO SKYROCKET YOUR EXISTENCE

By now you have become a true expert in the power of the Moon and you have already acquired the knowledge required to optimize its effects on your life. Below I am going to lay down the most effective rituals that have worked for me. These rituals will allow you to unlock your fullest potential, vibrating at the highest levels of frequencies to transform your entire life.

Unless you change your daily routine and let go of any past habits that have been dragging you down, you cannot expect to experience the magnitude of lunar energy. You will only get to a point and then keep wondering what you are doing wrong. You must modify your behavior accordingly and stop hindering the flow of energy into your life. It is time to get practical and see how your actions can indeed affect your progress, and either make or break your spiritual advancement.

As you will see, I have laid out a morning ritual which will help you boost your day, and project everything you want into the world. I have also created a special nighttime ritual to relax, rest, and be fully in tune with the Moon's energy. Feel free to make the necessary changes that reflect your own, personal preferences. You can add more meditations, rituals, spells, and other ways to find your inner balance.

Remember to be consistent in these rituals, as they will help you find that precious harmony you have been searching for all this time. Do not sabotage yourself by indulging in unhealthy habits that only bring you down and lower your vibrational frequencies. Instead, think smart and incorporate the right habits that allow you to unlock the purest form of lunar energy, welcoming all the blessings you desire in your life.

DAILY RITUAL FORMULA

So let's dive right in, and see how you can start your morning with an easy-to-follow ritual that skyrockets your existence and allows you to supercharge the rest of the day! First of all, make sure that you get enough sleep. I know that several moon phases might mess with your sleep patterns, but do try to relax and get an adequate amount of sleep. Otherwise, the following day you are going to be in a bad mood and you will not have the energy it takes to achieve greatness.

Take a few moments to make your bed and complete the first task of the day as early as possible. This will fill you with pride, as it represents an accomplishment of yours. It doesn't matter how trivial it may seem because it is indeed something you have completed successfully in your daily routine! Then open the windows and let the sunshine in, along with the fresh air and the soothing sounds of the morning. Of course, it would be ideal if you could pop out of your home and enjoy nature. However, even opening the shutters and allowing the new day's glow to bathe your bedroom helps you wake up naturally, and lifts your spirit. Take some deep breaths and appreciate the present moment, observing the sky to see if the Moon is still out there.

Brew some coffee or tea and prepare a healthy breakfast, as this will allow you to be mindful of your morning. Before doing that, it is important that you drink some water. You can make your own Moon water by charging it under the moonlight and drinking it first thing in the morning. In this way, you will be able to absorb the energy of the Moon and bring it with you into your day. Just dedicate a few minutes to enjoying your breakfast, sipping on this liquid bliss in a mug or a tall glass and reflecting on your day. Listen to your favorite music, light a scented candle, and enjoy being present.

As you can understand, the lunar cycle dictates different approaches to your daily ritual. So depending on the exact moon phase, you should then sit comfortably at your spiritual altar and get your journal out. If you are on the new moon, then you must set your intentions. Write down what you want to manifest during this lunar cycle and be as detailed as possible. Later on in the cycle, you can turn back to those intentions and figure out how to act towards accomplishing your goals. Once again, during the full moon, you should celebrate and be thankful. During the waning period, you must focus on releasing the tension and negativity, slowly accepting the ending of yet another lunar cycle.

Spend a few moments with your journal and be creative. You can try drawing or expressing whatever your heart desires

FULL MOON RITUAL MASTERY

on a piece of paper. Reflect on your thoughts and desires, visualizing them and making them part of your reality. If you close your eyes and visualize everything in which you wish to succeed in life, your mood will be lifted even more in an instant. You will be vibrating at higher frequencies, allowing for the Law of Attraction to grant you your wishes. This is a great way to start your day, picturing that you have already received these blessings into your life. While you are visualizing, you can repeat positive affirmations that enhance your experience. For instance, you can say, *I have abundance in my life, I feel blessed and full, my career has skyrocketed and my personal life gives me endless joy.* Even if you do not already have all those things in your life, try to see these things in your mind.

After having completed your visualization, it is time for some supercharging EFT sessions! This is especially important to do in the period right before the new moon, as this clears negativity and makes space for the new intentions you are about to set. Through EFT tapping, you stimulate different parts of your body by tapping your fingers on them to elevate vibration. In this way, you will release the tension and stress that has been piling up, clearing any blockages and allowing your blessings to set in.

You start at the top of your head, using two fingers to tap while repeating the following: *I am worthy. I release whatever no longer serves me. I welcome abundance in my life.* Move down to the center between your eyebrows, while sighing with relief. Continue by tapping the area of your face right below your eyes, repeating those positive affirmations. Of course, you can adjust them according to the exact moon phase to optimize your results and make the most of your intentions. Keep on tapping the upper lip, the chin and then your throat, the chest and under your armpits. After completing a full round, do this again until you feel comforted.

If you want, you can even write down your morning ritual

and stick it on your fridge, or keep it by your bedside table. You can stick it on your wall as a source of inspiration, decorated in a way that sparks joy and speaks right to your heart. Prepare a cute to-do list like the following:

- Create a welcoming atmosphere.
- Make my bed.
- Sip on some Moon water.
- Prepare my morning beverage and breakfast.
- Journal at my altar.
- Visualize my goals.
- Take time for EFT tapping.

This will be your morning guide towards a day filled with endless potential! Obviously, you can tweak this ritual as per your own preferences. Instead of visualization, you can step into a few moments of mindful meditation while listening to inspirational music. You can also add some yoga into the mix, if you wish to stretch and get your energy flowing. Otherwise, you can work out a little indoors or go out for a jog after this ritual is over. Whatever you do, do not put pressure on yourself! Let your moves flow naturally, aligning fully to the universe and surrendering to the energy of the Moon.

One more note before moving on to a wonderful nighttime ritual is about crystals. They can be amazing assets when used properly during the lunar cycle, and they can be charged or cleansed under the full moon. During the new moon, you can use black obsidian, labradorite, and black kyanite. The full moon calls for selenite, moonstone, and clear quartz. In between cycles, you can always use black tourmaline, clear quartz, and tourmalinated quartz for optimal results. See which of these crystals serve your purpose, and of course combine them with crystals that match your personality for the optimal results!

Nighttime Ritual

A full day has passed and you have finally returned home. I am sure you are feeling exhausted and the only thing you want is to relax. However, instead of crawling on the sofa and binge-watching a TV series, you can do so much more. You must remember that Moon mastery calls for your actions too! So dedicate some time to yourself, clearing your mind, and letting go of all negativity. I would advise you to shower in the evening, as the healing power of the water will purify your body and mind.

Another thing that allows you to make the most of your evening are Moon salutations, known as "Chandra Namasakar." In this exercise, you give thanks to the Moon and become part of its calming power. It is greatly helpful for you to do these Moon salutations at night, as they are channeling feminine divine energy from the Moon. So right before bed, if you want to embrace the lunar balance in your life, you must perform these yoga poses and fully relax.

First do the mountain pose. As you are standing up with your feet together, open your palms facing in front of you, and then proceed with the upward mountain. In this pose, you will bring your palms above your head and allow them to touch each other. Breathe deeply throughout these poses. Keeping your hands like that, slowly bend sideways at your waist, first to the left and then to the right. Only bend far enough to feel a slight stretch. This is the crescent pose. After this, we will go into the goddess pose. Take a step so that your feet are shoulder-width apart and turned outwards. Squat down low so that your knees are right above your ankles, creating a rectangular shape. Extend your arms out away from your body and bring them to a prayer mudra, with your thumb touching your middle finger, and your hands facing upwards.

Next, you should do the star pose. For this pose, stand up

and open your legs slightly. Hold your arms out to the side, in line with your shoulders, so that you create a star shape with your body. From there, bend at the waist and reach down, touching your left arm to your left foot without bending your knees, creating the triangle pose. When your left arm is down, your right arm will remain extended upwards and vice versa. Then, bring the second arm down to also touch that foot, to create the pyramid pose. From that pose, you can then bend your right knee back to touch the ground, extending the leg slightly. Your right foot and knee should be touching the ground, while your left leg should be bent in front of you with the knee facing upwards. Your arms should be stretched above your head, as you look up at your hands.

Our next pose involves a wide legged squat over the left leg. From the position you are in, bring your arms from above your head and all the way down touching the floor. Extend your right leg outwards from the right side of your body with your toes pointing up. Your left leg should be crouched in front of you. Rotate your left leg to the left side. In the end, this pose should have your palms pressed to the floor, your right leg extended with your toes pointing up, and your left leg folded to the side underneath your body.

Then do the whole routine on your other side, this time with your right foot. As you can imagine, you will follow the exact same pattern of poses on the opposite side, but in reverse order! Begin with the pyramid pose, the triangle pose, and the star pose, then the goddess pose and the crescent pose, before completing the cycle with the mountain pose. Finally, bring both your palms facing each other to the height of your chest and give thanks to the Moon, by repeating, *Namaste*.

This is a magnificent way for you to relax and become fully aligned with the Moon. The best way to perform this sequence of yoga poses is, of course, during the full moon and the new moon, but you are free to do this on a daily basis, if you feel like there is some harmony missing. Whenever you wish to relax and let go of the tension, reevaluating your life and bringing balance, Moon salutations can help you a great deal. Perform them mindfully and be grateful to the Moon for enabling you to reach your goals and welcome your blessings.

After that, you can prepare yourself some herbal or chamomile tea, and sit comfortably at your spiritual altar. Avoid any blue light for at least an hour before bedtime, and instead focus on your personal growth. Visualize your intentions, write in your journal and track your mood. Find things in your day that have made you feel good about yourself and reflect on them! You should be proud of your accomplishments, exuding positivity and elevating your frequencies. If you spend those last moments of your day comparing yourself to others and feeling lacking, then this is what you are going to project to the world.

AFTERWORD

You have made it to the end of this book and this fills me with great joy and satisfaction! I am sure that you have learned a lot about the power of the Moon and its cherished energy, and have gained a new, more spiritual perspective on life! In this book, I have put all my love into creating something that speaks right to your heart and allows you to claim your birthright. You have been blessed as a human being with a wealth of things, if you only reach out and grab them. The Moon will be right there by your side, whether you can see it or not. It is supporting you, helping you reach your goals and enjoy life exactly how you deserve.

In the book, I have explained the different moon phases and the way each of them affects you in your life. As soon as you fully comprehend the way the Moon works in combination with the rest of the cosmos, you will be able to unfold those mystical secrets of the universe and use them to your advantage! I have talked about the zodiac signs and how your astrological birth chart can influence your life on so many levels, provided that you know where to look. Next, I have referred to the emblematic Law of Attraction that dictates your life and defines what you receive from the world around you.

It has been a wonderful adventure, laying out these guided meditations that you can practice throughout the different moon phases. Some of them should be performed during the new moon, while others are ideal for the full moon, or even all throughout the lunar cycle. Just make sure to immerse yourself in the meditation and give your heart and soul into setting realistic intentions, so that you can watch them grow and become your new reality. Welcome change into your life, and be open and receptive to those glorious blessings. Have faith in the process, because it is based on the eternal power of the Moon and its overwhelming energy!

Finally, I have included a morning ritual you can perform every day to enhance the effectiveness of the Moon energy in your life. A nighttime ritual is also available, in order to give thanks to the Moon and increase your mental clarity, while letting go of the tension and releasing all negativity before going to sleep. If you are consistent and dedicate time to performing these rituals, then you will welcome change and see your entire life transform, finally forming exactly the way you have been dreaming of. I am looking forward to communicating with you in my other books as well, filling the missing pieces of spirituality one by one.

By taking initiative and choosing this book, you have already completed the first and most important step towards improving your life! You had an amazing idea and you now have all the things you need, in order to make wonders happen. I am confident that you are going to achieve greatness sooner than you have ever anticipated. There are so many wonderful things waiting for you to open and receive in your life! You are ready, and it is time to welcome abundance, pure joy, and success supercharged by lunar energy. Aren't you excited about what comes next? Just reach out and claim what has been destined for you by the wise universe! I believe in you and you are entitled to all the blessings of the world. So go on, conquer them, and enjoy every moment of your life from now on... you deserve it!

REFERENCES

Ackerman, C. E. (2018, May 2). *Self-Fulfilling Prophecy in Psychology: 10 Examples and Definition (+PDF)*. PositivePsychology.com. https://positivepsychology.com/self-fulfilling-prophecy/

adege. (2018). *Lunar Eclipse Blood Moon Full* [Photograph]. Pixabay. https://pixabay.com/photos/lunar-eclipse-blood-moon-moon-3568801/

Bessi. (2015). *Tree Lake Stars* [Photograph]. Pixabay. https://pixabay.com/photos/tree-lake-stars-reflection-water-838667/

Candiix. (2018). *Moon Couple Blue* [Photograph]. Pixabay. https://pixabay.com/photos/moon-couple-blue-love-in-love-3059324/

Choi, C. Q. (2017, September 8). *Moon Facts: Fun Information About the Earth's Moon*. Space.com. https://www.space.com/55-earths-moon-formation-composition-and-orbit.html

Comfreak. (2016). *Earth Moon Space* [Photograph]. Pixabay. https://pixabay.com/illustrations/earth-moon-space-space-travel-1151659/

DanaTentis. (2017). *Woman Brunette Lying Down* [Photograph]. Pixabay. https://pixabay.com/photos/woman-brunette-lying-down-rest-2003647/

Dropic, A. (2018). *Science Nature Moon* [Photograph]. Pixabay. https://pixabay.com/photos/science-nature-moon-mountain-3191080/

enriquelopezgarre. (2020). *Landscape Cave Moon* [Photograph]. Pixabay. https://pixabay.com/photos/landscape-cave-moon-twilight-night-5563684/

enriquelopezgarre. (2020). *Landscape Night Star* [Photograph]. Pixabay. https://pixabay.com/photos/landscape-night-star-phases-5186058/

fietzfotos. (2020). *Moon Night Plastic* [Photograph]. Pixabay. https://pixabay.com/photos/moon-night-plastic-crescent-5224745/

Free-Photos. (2014). *Tea Cup Rest* [Photograph]. Pixabay. https://pixabay.com/photos/tea-cup-rest-calm-afternoon-381235/

Free-photos. (2015). *Milky Way Stars Man* [Photograph]. Pixabay. https://pixabay.com/photos/milky-way-stars-man-silhouette-1023340/

GabbyConde. (2020). *Crystals Selenite Stones* [Photograph]. Pixabay. https://pixabay.com/photos/crystals-selenite-stones-stone-4831221/

Grover, N. (2021, January 27). *Lunar cycle has distinct effect on sleep, study suggests*. The Guardian. https://www.theguardian.com/lifeandstyle/2021/jan/27/lunar-cycle-has-distinct-effect-on-sleep-study-suggests

Hickey, H. (2016, January 29). *Moon's tidal forces affect amount of rainfall on Earth*. UW News. https://www.washington.edu/news/2016/01/29/phases-of-the-moon-affect-amount-of-rainfall/

KELLEPICS. (2020). *Fantasy Moon Girl* [Photograph]. Pixabay. https://pixabay.com/illustrations/fantasy-moon-girl-night-bank-5316369/

Lopez Simpson, S. (2017, October 6). *9 Habits to Manifest Your Dreams Using the Law of Attraction*. Mindbodygreen. https://www.mindbodygreen.com/0-16150/9-habits-to-manifest-your-dreams-using-the-law-of-attraction.html

mcbeaner. (2017). *Aurora Moon Scotland* [Photograph]. Pixabay. https://pixabay.com/illustrations/aurora-moon-scotland-beach-2069242/

MiraCosic. (2015). *Astrology Divination Chart* [Photograph]. Pixabay. https://pixabay.com/photos/astrology-divination-chart-993127/

mistockshop. (2016). *Planner Journal Notebook* [Photograph]. Pixabay. https://pixabay.com/photos/planner-journal-notebook-organizer-1873485/

Sinnott, R. W. (2017, September 14). *Find the Phase of the Moon*. Sky & Telescope. https://skyandtelescope.org/observing/the-phase-of-the-moon/

spirit1111. (2017). *Moon Full Moonlight* [Photograph]. Pixabay. https://pixabay.com/photos/moon-full-moon-moonlight-super-moon-2285627/

terimakasiho. (2019). *Chest Treasure Pirate* [Photograph]. Pixabay. https://pixabay.com/photos/chest-treasure-pirate-money-box-4051166/

vitavalka. (2015). *Clock Historical Prague* [Photograph]. Pixabay. https://pixabay.com/photos/clock-historical-prague-city-signs-1096054/

Willgard. (2018). *Dreams Heaven Stairs Fantasy* [Photograph]. Pixabay. https://pixabay.com/photos/dreams-heaven-stairs-fantasy-woman-3745156/

World History Edu. (2021, May 4). *Khonsu: Ancient Egyptian God of the Moon and Time*. World History Edu. https://www.worldhistoryedu.com/khonsu-ancient-egyptian-god-of-the-moon-and-time/

❧ II ☙
SPIRITUAL CLEANSING

Soul Cleansing Secrets No One Talks
About & How To Cleanse Negative Energy
From Your House In 7 Days

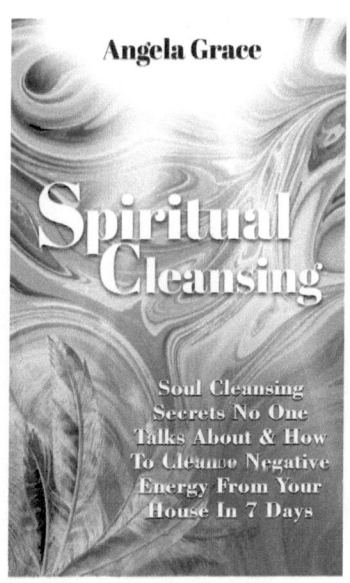

INTRODUCTION

Do you want to cleanse your home and your soul from any negative energy, lifting your spirit and rejuvenating your senses? It can be hard resorting to your home as a safe haven, only to experience energy drainage and constant agony. You deserve to purify the atmosphere, allowing yourself to feel awesome all the time in an inspiring, welcoming environment. There is no place for clogged energy, negative spirits and clutter.

In this book, you will find out how to get rid of the evil eye and lift any curses or hex you have been the victim to. Unfortunately, there are a lot of forces out there wishing to do you harm. You should not let them; instead, you need to build a force field of defense around you, so that you are immune to such threats. There are easy to follow instructions, rituals and routines that you can do, so as to enhance your ability to steer clear from negative entities, earthbound spirits and ghosts.

Whether you have just moved into a new house and want to dispose of the energy from the previous tenant, or you want to start fresh, I will show you the way to achieve your goals. I will guide you step by step towards fully comprehending what you are up against. Only by knowing who the enemy is can you live up to the challenge and face them. What does a curse feel like? How can you tell that you have been the victim of the evil eye? Why do people feel jealous of you and how can you armor yourself?

You will learn more about the aura and its distinct, colorful layers. This is one of the major means of protection for you. The aura has been scientifically proven to exist, as part of your entity. In fact, it surrounds you with a powerful source of energy. In this book, you will see how to elevate your electromagnetic field and attract happiness and prosperity, rather than feelings of sadness and despair. You will be able to open your spirit channels and expand your aura, absorbing negative energy and avoiding psychic vampires and other entities distracting you from your higher purpose in life.

More than that, you are going to learn how to protect your home from any negative energy. There are hostile entities, negative energies, uninvited guests, ghosts and even extraterrestrial implants that you should encounter. This is of paramount importance, as you are meant to feel safe and comfortable within your personal space. When someone compromises that feeling of security, your entire world crumbles down. By using simple ingredients and effective techniques you can use at home, you can suck out all bad energy and create an uplifting environment, where you can be happy and thrive.

Get in touch with your past lives, as they can be of paramount importance to you. By connecting with them and accepting them without judgment, you can do something that most people would never have the chance to do. These past lives are part of who you are, but they do not define you completely. If you have suffered from a trauma in a past life, you can travel back in time and learn more details about it. In this way, you will be able to come to terms with the reality and resolve that endless conundrum you have been dealing with. Instead of swirling in the same vortex again and again, you can sigh with relief and get ready to move on with your current life. On the contrary, you will realize that you can change your course and reach higher levels of divinity in this life.

This book will also help you make the most of your inner energy levels. Cleanse your chakras, ensuring that your energy flows undisrupted. You do not want to see any clogged energy, as this would mean that there is something wrong with you and your body. Make use of modern techniques that can energize your body, enabling you to vibrate at a higher frequency that promotes positive feelings. Benefit from guided meditations that target these specific aspects of your being. Get accustomed to techniques such as TRE, EFT tapping and Qi Jong to promote your well-being.

Finally, get to cleanse your home from bad vibes in just 7 days. A week is more than enough for you to change your life. You will have the opportunity to cleanse your personal space and keep all those dangerous, negative entities out of reach. It doesn't take a lot of time to get these results, either. By using the power of archangels, your guardian angels and your spiritual guides, banish any negative spirit or entity, along with stagnant energy that has been dragging you down. You deserve so much more than that!

My Own Journey

Let me tell you a few things about me and how I came to be involved in spirituality. In my life, I have always been curious to explore the unknown. As a child, I used to ask a lot of questions and delve deeper to get answers that made me feel safe. Growing up in an amazingly loving environment, I was blessed to experience happiness and creativity, hope and optimism for the future. My world was ready to be unfolded before my eyes, opening up a wealth of opportunities.

When I moved out and got into an apartment far from the place I had been raised, all that was suddenly gone. My world lacked balance and I blamed myself for that. I thought I was responsible for all the turbulence I experienced. Every time I walked into my home, the very moment I got through the threshold, I felt exhausted. It seemed as if my inner spirit had abandoned me. No longer did I have the will to create, to wonder, to investigate and expand my horizons. All I wanted was to curl up on the sofa and watch TV until I fell asleep.

However, I could not even find peace and rest during sleep. It was a never-ending nightmare for me. Sometimes I would feel lethargic, but would not fall asleep until early morning. And even when I did, I would wake up feeling equally drained of energy. Have you ever been in a situation, when you know you want something and still can never catch a break and actually get it? I was in a pitfall and I did not know how to get out of this mess. Everything was put on hold, as I could not perform my best. In fact, fear crept inside me and made me worry about what my life was going to be like.

On a bright note, I discovered crystals, energy healing, & spirituality after being introduced to healing crystals by my friend Linda. She was one of the first persons to inspire me towards following that path into enlightenment. I was amazed at the things I heard from her. She spoke about negative spirits and entities from the past that can be trapped within a space on earth, tormenting those around them. She explained to me the importance of spiritual cleansing and self-healing processes. At first, I have to admit that I was a bit skeptical about all that. My mind resisted the thought of someone else being responsible for my emotional and physical ordeal. However, as soon as my mind opened to that possibility and I performed a deep cleanse of my home and body, I was stunned by the results.

Having experienced such great improvement in the way I felt, I was convinced that I was hexed and my home was dominated by negative energy. After getting rid of those entities that undermined my happiness, everything changed. I could now fall asleep peacefully and sleep through the night. I felt filled with energy in the morning, opening the blinds to let the sunlight bathe my apartment. It felt like I finally woke up from a nightmare and I could continue on my path to reach my goals. Once I stumbled upon the magic of soul cleansing and cleansing negative energy from home, it affected my own life and allowed me to thrive. My journey has brought me here, eager to pass on my knowledge to those around me and hopefully motivate them to change their life.

I have written several other books in this niche, all of which opt to give you a new perspective, an innovative look at spirituality. *"Energy Healing Made Easy," "Protect Your Energy," "Crystals Made Easy," "Feminine Energy Awakening," "Manifesting for Women"* and "Reiki Made Easy" are all parts of the same journey. They motivate you to align with your energy, reach out to your divine self and discover the mysteries of the universe. You have the power to do that and I have been blessed to know how to help you succeed.

Join Spiritual Cleansing

Spiritual cleansing can transform your life forever, as long as you have faith. You do not have to feel oppressed, settling for negative thoughts and emotions. It is in your hands to elevate your vibrational frequencies, discarding anything that has been dragging you in the mud. You need to spread your wings and fly away, in searches of new uncharted lands. Why would you ever want to take things for granted, surrounded by disbelief and continuous compromise?

Once you purify your psyche, your spirit and your home, you will instantly find that precious relief you have been searching for. It will open a new world of possibilities for you, as you will no longer be kept down by negative entities that wish nothing but to harm you. As long as you adhere to the easy and simple guidelines I have laid out for you in this book, you can be sure that your world will be an entirely different place from now on.

Do not let others suck your energy and withhold you from accomplishing your higher intentions in life. You have been destined for great things. Therefore, you should not be consumed in a never-ending cycle of negativity. This weakens you over time, preventing you from enjoying life to the fullest. You cannot have that. Not when there are abundant benefits to discovering the secrets of spirituality.

I have gathered these secrets in this book for you to apply in your life right away. Do not waste any more time. Let the power of the divine bless you from within, shedding light on your darkest fears and casting away negative energy. Join me in this endeavor to transform your existence, expand your perspective of life and actually be happy. Be present in the moment, appreciate who you are and what you have been blessed with in life, finally getting what you deserve.

Keep reading this book if you are intrigued about the endless possibilities of your mind, your body and soul. Start studying and prepare yourself to get dazzled. There are a lot of wonderful things that you can do, rather than sit idle and expect negative spirits and malevolent presences to leave on their own. You have the power to make them go, whether they want to or not. It is all in your hands, as long as you know which buttons to push. With just a few tweaks here and there, you will see your whole life change course. Good luck and stay blessed!

CHAPTER 1: YOU, YOUR FAMILY, YOUR PETS, YOUR FOOD, THE TREES OUTSIDE AND EVERYTHING ELSE ARE ALL UNIVERSAL ENERGY

Look around you. What do you see? The leaves on the trees, the gentle breeze and the smells of blooming flowers, the sun rays bathing the houses, the birds chirping blissfully in the background. This is a majestic landscape out in the countryside. Not all of us have been blessed with such scenery in our daily routine. So maybe what you see is bustling streets, cars stuck in traffic, people rushing to finish their work for the day, neon lights. Even though these are entirely different surroundings, they do have something in common. They are ultimately Geometry in perfect alignment.

According to Greek mythology, Atlas was given the exhausting task to hold the globe in his hands. This maintained universal balance, although it was obviously excruciating for the Greek tragic hero. Many poets have praised Atlas for his perseverance and selflessness. If he let go of the celestial spheres, the world would collapse in a matter of seconds. Everything would turn into dust, even the slightest wrong move of a single person. (Wikipedia Contributors, 2019) This myth has obviously been discredited by modern

FULL MOON RITUAL MASTERY

Science. However, it teaches us that balance is much more difficult to achieve than we think.

The universe has been created in absolute harmony and you are a part of this global masterpiece. But what does this mean? How can the world function properly, rather than fall into chaos? The answer lies within the concept of universal energy. There is energy hidden within every single one of us. Energy dictates our movements and ensures harmony all around. Otherwise, it would be impossible to coordinate our entities and avoid continuous crashes.

What power guides the universe? There is an exciting theory that explains it quite accurately. Based on the Constructal theory, the design of the atom and the cosmos are the same in their very core. They are almost identical, just like replicas. The way a molecule emits energy and vibrates is the same as that of the cosmos. Energy is infinite and flows through every being, every part of the universe, everything we perceive through our senses. What changes is the complexity of the design. Smaller structures require simpler architecture, which is perfectly understandable (Bejan & Lorente, 2010).

We live in a pulsing and vibrating universe of advanced harmony. You are vibrating also, as part of the universe. Everything in the universe is energy, but it is spread on different levels. Just take a moment and imagine the vast power of energy in a single atom. There is a massive energy that flows through you, through me and through everything in between. A single molecule could as well light up a whole town for a day, should its energy be concentrated and repurposed.

If the tiniest living organism contains an immense quantity of energy, then what happens with individuals? What happens with groups of people, communities, entire cities or countries or even continents? How much energy does that amount to? The numbers are jaw-dropping. Although it is impossible to quantify such energies, it is fair to conclude that there is inexhaustible energy all around us.

If you are determined to clear negative energy and create a positive self and home environment, it is imperative that you understand how the universe works. Otherwise, you will not be able to succeed in your endeavor. Therefore, it is crucial to comprehend that you are not isolated, operating independently from anything around you. Instead, you are swimming in an ocean of energy. This energy is inexhaustible.

The Universal Energy of Frequency and Vibration

"The field is the sole governing agency of the particle," as Albert Einstein has described most eloquently. An invisible plexus of energy is everywhere, creating matter and preserving it. All the cells and molecules are dictated by the same principles and governed by the same power, forming each creature and sustaining it for life (freeAgent42, 2018).

Quantum Physics has attempted to explain the principles governing the universe. Subatomic particles adhere to specific rules, which define the world around us. Between the nucleus of every atom and the electrons surrounding it, there is electromagnetic energy. This is invaluable, as it shows there is a continuous flow of energy surrounding everything in the world. Rather than staying still and concrete, reality is ever-flowing. Whether we perceive it or not, the universe is constantly changing based on that very energy.

Energy is everywhere, vibrating at a specific speed to influence reality. When we listen to a single sound, our ears translate vibration. The same happens with all our senses. This is the way to perceive the world. Without this movement, we would be unable to comprehend what lies ahead. Reality has been structured through vibrating pulses. Since we are part of existence, we are also frequency generators. We emit energy to the world, influencing it at a distinct level.

What is even more enticing of a thought is the fact that we can change the world, according to our frequency. The Law of Attraction suggests that an individual's inner state affects the surroundings, eventually attracting the things that are manifested through their thoughts and feelings. This is a shocking revelation, as it allows people to transform reality by changing the way they feel (Corbin, n.d.).

The cosmos is within you. You can shape it any way you want it, as long as you modify your inner self accordingly. Do you seek health, prosperity, fame and money in your future? By manifesting them from within, you make sure that you attract them into your life. On the other hand, if you focus on negative emotions, then this is what you are going to attract. It is a natural course of events, which you are responsible for through the Law of Attraction.

This is an amazing feeling, being able to influence the universe through your own power. As soon as you comprehend how it works, you will be able to attract all those wonderful things in life. You will have the opportunity to devote yourself to your true purpose, without the distractions that have been dragging you down all this time. Now you will be free to create, explore, inspire and motivate others to join your path.

You Are Part of the World
The emotional focus of people in a single event could form universal consciousness. This is how powerful vibration

is. When a natural disaster occurs, there is a spike in the global energy that resembles the spike following an earthquake. People get emotionally affected when hearing about a negative event and this emotion is manifested through a change in the global energy. We are part of something great, parts of a Whole that lives and breathes in unity.

That being said, it makes sense that all living beings within the universe communicate with each other. You can talk to the spiritual entity of all things, as they can talk to you. This is the concept of universal intelligence. Take for example the work of Japanese researcher Masaru Emoto. He experimented with water, exposing different containers to different emotions and stimuli. The results were amazing. Water that had been transformed into impressive molecule formations, whereas water subjected to negative stimulants became ugly and disfigured (Pitkanen, 2018).

When energy remains stagnant, things around it start to wither and fall apart. Life is maintained only through vibration. Once the energy is blocked, this vibrational system is disrupted. The outcome is truly heartbreaking. There can be no life without vibration. Your existence depends on the frequency at which you vibrate. You can change that frequency by charging yourself with the power of items, individuals and emotions that emit elevated levels of vibration.

Only through unconditional love can we achieve that connection with the universe and reach harmony. Forging a connection with this universal consciousness is of paramount importance. Although it sounds awesome, there are hurdles getting in the way of making that happen. In a turbulent environment filled with distractions, focusing on one's spiritual self becomes a lot harder.

By accepting that the same energy flows through everything around us, we instantly become stronger. We fully comprehend how the universe works, charging all things with positive energy and enabling them to reach their higher purpose. You are part of the world, hence you should opt at charging your body and your environment as high as possible. In this way, you will get the opportunity to attract positive things in life, through the Law of Attraction.

Connecting to the Universe Checklist

Below, I have created a quick checklist of some of the things you need to consider to draw your conclusion as to whether or not you are connected to the universe. Answer truthfully, as this will affect your further development. There is no reason to blame yourself, if you find out that you are less connected than anticipated. On the contrary, it is great that you have found out soon enough, so that you can align your energy and restore your profound connection with the cosmos.

- What is your relationship with animals? Do you have a pet? Do you love animals and interacting with them?
- Do you enjoy being outdoors? Do you often go on excursions, taking the opportunity to discover true gems of nature?
- Are you drawn to astronomy? Do you spend time looking at the stars in the sky? Do you read about the planets and the moon?
- Do you often find yourself in a "deja vu" state, when you think that you have had the same experience in a different life (or maybe in a parallel universe)?
- Do you recycle? What do you do to help the environment? Are you a volunteer or do you ignore the imminent dangers for the planet and our survival?
- Are you interested in weather forecasts? Are you

more focused on the prediction than the actual weather conditions?
- What is your relationship with technology? Have you developed an addiction to electronic devices and the web, or have you managed to maintain a healthy relationship?
- Do you think it is probable that you have lived different lives in the past, or do you believe that we only live once?
- Do you often resort to medications even for mild discomfort, or do you prefer alternative medicine?
- Do you have any indoor plants? Does your home have a balcony? If so, do you have plants there? Or do you live in a house with a garden?

Remember that there are no right or wrong answers here. This checklist should only be used as a point of reference, in order to realize how attached you are to nature and the cosmos around you. Do you believe that you are connected to the world through a mystical, invisible cord? No matter what your answers have been, it is in your hand to change your attitude towards nature and the world.

13

CHAPTER 2: MEET YOUR ADVERSARIES; THE EVIL EYE, NEGATIVE ENERGY AND DARK FORCES

The evil eye, or malevolent gaze, has been widely accepted as a concept ever since antiquity. All over the world, there are many different words describing the very same thing; an individual's envy may interfere with the good fortune of another individual. Many people believe that this is nothing more than superstition. However, it is a matter of causality.

Have you ever found yourself in a position, when someone else has looked at you in contempt? What has that caused you to feel? I am sure this gaze has affected you for a while, or even for an entire day. The art of seduction lies within the power of a single look. People use it to become more attractive, lure, or potentially manipulate others. Through subtle manners of action, a look can get you what you want or distract you from your goals.

When someone is jealous of you, they will most probably react badly even without them knowing. Their gaze might send negative vibes your way, affecting your existence. Envy is a severe negative emotion, preventing an individual from honestly being happy for the blessings of another person.

There are people who envy others subconsciously, since they directly compare them to their own life. What they are deprived of, they cannot accept to see in others. This can be a slippery slope, as there will always be something you do not have.

It is important to note that there are various references to the evil eye in spiritual books, as well as the Holy Scriptures. Hence, it should not be considered as a paganist concept that holds no ground. More than that, there are ceremonial rituals in many religions all over the world aiming at removing the evil eye from the person who has become a victim to its overwhelming power (Bledsoe, 2013).

If you are determined to cast away the evil eye, what you need to do first is become aware of its existence. Unless you acknowledge that it is there, you won't be able to fight it off effectively. Imagine you are preparing yourself for a job interview. You are advised to wear a suit, so as to increase the chances of getting the job. Where does the causality lie in this example? You cannot possibly believe that by dressing smart you can impress the HR department. What you can do is become aware of what you are wearing and acting accordingly. Your behavior will in turn reflect your confidence, leading to a significant increase in your chances to succeed.

Wearing a talisman against the evil eye works like that. You become aware of the threat that is related to the malevolent gaze. More than that, you let others know that you are aware of this threat. A person who is about to cast you a curse will think twice upon noticing that piece of jewelry that shields you against such dangers. That being said, a simple amulet may not be enough to keep the evil eye away from you. It is going to help you, though, as part of a holistic approach of identifying the evil eye as a curse and protecting yourself against it.

You need to know your adversaries, before being able to

rise to the challenge and confront them. Learn how to spot the warning signs of the evil eye, in order to realize when you need help. See through the curses cast upon you, so that you can act fast and lift them prior to affecting you dearly. Defend yourself, creating a protective wall that does not allow threats to penetrate its interior.

What Does a Curse Feel Like?

Are you wondering if you have become the victim of the evil eye, or another curse or hex? Do you feel like you can never catch a break? Are you constantly miserable, failing in everything you do? Is there an outside force preventing you from reaching out to your dreams? This is no magic, unlike what many people might claim. Someone does not drain you directly of your energy. It doesn't work like that. On the contrary, it is the impact of negative energy cast upon you, making your life more difficult. This is the curse, which can interfere with your well-being and turn your existence into an ordeal.

I know this all goes against what you have been taught in your life so far. You have been used to sending positive energy to others, praying for them and hoping that they are happy, healthy and accomplished. Your sole intention has always been to spark joy in other people's lives. How can another being seek the entire opposite thing for you? Is it true that there are entities out there undermining your well-being?

Curses are real, because you believe in them. Why do people cast curses in the first place? Curses are meant to bring chaos into your life. However, there is a widespread misconception about the way they are cast to someone. You may believe that there is a whole ritual behind curses. There are rituals, as well as prayers to malicious powers. This is a conscious effort to send out negative energy. It happens intentionally and it is meant to harm you. At the same time, though, there are many curses cast unintentionally. Mothers can cast a curse on their children, siblings can cast a curse on one another, even people who are meant to compliment you can do so without them knowing. It is less common than the traditional aspect of the malevolent eye, but it can happen.

Wishing bad things is more common than what you may think. Take a moment and picture a busy street in the middle of the day. You are driving, when another driver starts swearing. They are calling you bad names, simply because they want to drive past you. Just the thought of you standing in the way and distracting them from their goal is enough to curse. That negative energy takes its toll on you, as you are feeling exhausted because of that incident. Well, it is not by chance. The same happens at the supermarket, when people fight over a bottle of milk or the last candy bar by the cashier. They fight over Sports, Politics, current affairs and so much more.

That being said, some people spend their life never worrying about being cursed. They never think twice about it, as this is not something that usually comes up as a topic for discussion. It usually takes a huge shock for someone to start questioning their life. After hitting rock bottom, it is in our nature to contemplate all the things we have done, in a desperate need of answers. What has led us here and what has made us fail? Is it our own incompetence, our lack of determination, or is it something way beyond our grasp? Oddly enough, a curse is the culprit in many cases.

Cords of attachment bind your own negative feelings with those of others. You must be familiar with duality as a concept. Action comes with the respective form of reaction. Since we can send out love, compassion and light, it is only fair that we are able to do the exact opposite. It is within people's powers to send distress, pain and agony to others. Obviously, you need to be aware that by sending specific emotions, you attract them right back to you. So basically, whoever wishes negative things for others usually suffers even more.

When you receive the negative impact of a curse, your body's frequency absorbs it. As a result, your vibrations change radically. They become lower, which in turn leads to creating negative situations and attracting negative emotions —The perfect vicious cycle. Sometimes, earthbound spirits might join this downward spiral. They cling on to you, while having unresolved issues on their own.

Does a curse affect everyone in the same way, or are some people immune to such threats? Why are some people more susceptible to curses? First of all, people who believe in the evil eye and curses are those who get affected the most. However, ignoring the power of curses will not have a direct impact on the victims. They will still be cursed, they will still suffer, but they will most likely not connect the dots to realize what has been the cause of their ordeal.

Furthermore, being in a vulnerable state within your life helps you become more susceptible to curses. If things go really well for you, if you are in a loving relationship, if you get pure satisfaction out of your work and interaction with others and feel complete, then your shield has been lifted. You can keep those threats at bay far more efficiently. On the other hand, when you are feeling down and you are constantly doubting yourself, if you are unhappy in your relationship or feel trapped professionally, then your guard cracks open.

This all boils down to your vibration. When you emit vibration at lower frequencies, you attract negative things. You attract the evil eye and you motivate others to cast a curse on you. In times of big transitions, this phenomenon can become even more intense. These negative entities feed on your fear. When something big happens in your life, even if it is very good for you, it brings out insecurity. Even if you have just been promoted with a significantly big raise in your salary, you still feel afraid of what is going to happen next. This will be interpreted as weakness, attracting negativity.

Cast Curses Away

There are many different techniques out there to help you remove a curse. Whatever you do, you must be really committed to that. Do not let any distractions lead you astray. Then, you should have someone you trust, a friend or a spiritual guide, by your side. This will help you maintain your focus, while increasing your own power to remove negative spirits and curses from your body and home.

First of all, you can take a white, yellow or black candle and hold it in your palms. Look at it carefully, focusing your gaze on its material. While you are doing that, visualize that you are sending all the negative energy from the curse in this candle. Bring out the emotions associated with the curse, including your fear, anxiety and despair. Along with that, recall all the manifestations of this curse, as far as you know of. For instance, has the curse resulted in losing a precious belonging of yours? Has it made you sprain your ankle? After having concentrated for a few minutes, get that candle and let it burn somewhere without distractions and without blowing it out.

Alternatively, you can use the freezer spell. Just keep in mind that this spell is only effective if you know who has cast the curse on you. Write down the name of the person who has cursed you on a piece of paper. Then, take the paper and put it in a mason jar. Fill the jar with water and place it in the freezer. You can also use the person's picture or a personal item of theirs. The concept is quite simple, as through this spell you have the opportunity to freeze the energy of the curse. At the same time, it creates physical distance between this person and yourself.

In order to get rid of a curse, any type of energy healing will help you out. Reiki, aura cleansing and angelic energy will allow you to lift a curse. Nevertheless, you will need someone else to perform that energy healing on you. You have been affected by the curse, therefore you might be blindsided by it and not be able to remove it like you should. Alternatively, you can ask the person who has come to heal your energy to pray for you. In this way, you can join forces and amplify the energy you both generate. You can then remove a curse far more easily than you would by praying on your own. After all, there is strength in others!

CHAPTER 3: AURA MASTERY, WHAT YOU NEED TO KNOW TO MANIFEST A JOYFUL EXISTENCE

The aura is the illuminating electromagnetic energy that surrounds your body. It is like a protective blanket that follows your exact shape, formed to connect you to the world. To describe it more accurately, I would say the aura is egg-shaped and subtly colorful. As you become more aware of its presence, you get to realize how vibration actually works. You fully comprehend the importance of clearing the negative energy and get in touch with your inner balance.

Essentially, the aura is a vibrating electromagnetic field that surrounds all living creatures. There are 7 different aura layers in the energy body, placed one inside the other. Think of an onion's interior. It consists of different layers, which become thicker as you get further away from the core. They transmit information from the body to the direct external environment. Each layer has a different vibration and is directly linked to a distinct chakra energy center. The outer layers are higher in vibration, although each layer has its own role.

Never underestimate the value of a single energy layer. Since they vibrate at their unique frequencies, they are irreplaceable. They blend together in harmony, creating the individual's aura. A healthy body oozes with balanced energy and this can be shown through a rainbow-colored aura, balanced with a variety of chromatic shades and without any distortions. Always keep in mind that the aura is dynamic, meaning that it can change at any time, depending on the way a person is feeling and what they are thinking.

Learning about the essence of the aura is necessary, in order to comprehend the importance of balancing one's energetic fields. Electromagnetic energy is everywhere, affecting even the tiniest molecule in the universe. Energy creates and sustains life, providing an indestructible bond between the physical and the spiritual world. If you are determined to improve your life on all levels, you cannot ignore or underestimate the meaning of energy. Instead, by embracing the aura and enabling yourself to purify its different layers, you will notice a remarkable change in the way you feel.

Later in the book I will show you how to cleanse auras and give step by set instructions, so that you make the most of their amazing potential. Remember that clearing your energy and the negative energy in your home is of the essence for a joyful life. But first of all, after having grasped their meaning and where they come from, it is only fair that we move forward with distinguishing the different layers of auras. In this way, you will have the chance to address any red flags depicted by your aura. Think of them as indicators of your physical and spiritual health.

If you want to see your aura on a piece of paper, then you can search for aura photography. This is a controversial technique, but you can use it to analyze the different colors, shapes and sizes depicted in the photo. Even if you are prepared for what you are about to see, it can still be shocking to observe your electromagnetic field like that. It is even more disturbing, of course, if you find out that your aura is disfigured. This means that you have some sort of energetic imbalance that you need to take care of, in order to restore a healthy and lively aura.

Layers of Aura

As we discussed, there are 7 different layers of the aura, associated with the 7 chakra energy centers within your body. The first 3 aura layers, the ones closest to your physical self, represent the physical plane. The astral body reflects the astral plane, whereas the last 3 aura layers represent the spiritual plane. All those layers work together and aim at providing the precious balance of your entity.

- Etheric body: This is found right after the physical body, extending up to 2 inches in size. It is the layer closest to your physical presence and acts as a mediator that transfers the energies between the aura and the body itself. The etheric body is dense and thick, blue in color, resembling the physical body but still having a higher vibration. If you look carefully, you can see this layer with a naked eye. The etheric body is connected to the root chakra. It offers liveliness and structure, highlighting even slight abnormalities that may develop into disease.
- Emotional body: As its name suggests, this is the aura responsible for the emotional balance of the body. You store the emotional energy there. It is connected with the sacral chakra and it can get various different colors. What is interesting about this layer is the fact that when you get stressed, darker holes seem to appear on its surface. This highlights most eloquently how great the impact of

emotional distress can be on your well-being. It is almost as if your aura gets traumatized by negative emotions.

- Mental body: Moving further apart from the physical body, up to 8 inches, we find the mental body. The mental body is associated with the solar plexus chakra. It is bright yellow in color and it is mostly concentrated around the head and the neck. This happens because it is related to the mental processes, reflecting one's personal power. An individual's attitude is affected by this aura. Self-doubts can be catastrophic for the balance of this layer, which may lead to fogginess, clouded judgment and a lack of mental clarity.
- Astral body: As we are moving further away from the physical body, about twelve inches, this aura shows your ability to love and be loved unconditionally. It is light pink and its health is promoted through healthy, intense relationships. The astral body is linked with the heart chakra, connecting the three inner and outer layers of the aura. Once you reach this layer, you are introduced to the astral plane.
- Etheric double: The etheric double is located after the astral body and reaches 18 inches from your physical body. Its color varies and it is connected with the throat chakra. Basically, it mirrors the etheric body and therefore reflects the aspects of your physical existence. This layer protects everything you hold dear in the world. As a result, negative thinking will lead to imbalances and a lack of confidence. If the imbalance is prolonged, then you are at risk of sickness manifestations.
- Celestial body: This is otherwise known as the

hologramatic and is associated with the third eye chakra. It is the aura associated with enlightenment and is responsible for higher intellectual knowledge. You can see it at a distance of up to 24 inches from your physical self, in a dovey white color. Celestial body symbolizes your consciousness and the way you perceive things in reality. It is also where your imagination sparks and your intuition is developed on a more spiritual level. Once you strengthen this layer enough, you can connect with the spiritual world and communicate with your divine self.

- Ketheric template: Extending up to three feet from your physical body, this is the seventh and ultimate layer of your aura. It holds a deep connection with the crown chakra, which allows you to understand everything. You can see it in pure gold color. This layer holds the divine knowledge and promotes universal power and consciousness. All the experiences gained so far are manifested through a thorough understanding of the world. In addition, the ketheric template enables you to reach into your soul and look through your past lives. Negative emotions will lead to doubts about your higher self, your purpose in life and the divine.

These layers of the aura work together, so as to protect you from all harm. They are like a shield, which prevents negative energies and entities from penetrating your defense. If, however, even one of these layers does not function properly, then the whole structure fails to work as it should. This is when you are most vulnerable to those threats. In order to restore the balance, you need to cleanse your aura and at the same time recharge it. In this way, you will ensure that it is always thick enough to protect your body and strong enough to keep any negative energies at bay.

Even though the aura is not made of any material, you can in fact observe it. You just need to look closely. You can also touch it and comprehend its presence all around you. Of course, you cannot hold it in your hands like you would hold a jacket or a key. Still, it is fascinating to understand electromagnetism on a different level. This is not just Physics, it is every person's reality.

How to See Auras

Auras come in many colors, but the exact colors you see will reveal certain aspects of an individual's true self. As soon as you see the aura's colors, you will be able to draw conclusions as per one's personality and quality. Blue color characterizes an idealist, who adheres to the moral codes and principles. As the color of the heart chakra, green reflects compassion, trust and love. If you are looking for a loyal person by your side, search for a bright green aura. Red is the color of courage, strength and energy. At the same time, however, it displays anger and a deeper will to destroy everything.

A caring person who opts at maintaining peace and harmony in their relationships is characterized by the light pink color of their aura. Yellow color is usually found in teachers and those who wish to pass on their knowledge to others. It is also typical of communication. Orange is the color of creativity and reflects a person's level of independence. If you are searching for spiritual traits, then purple is the color to look for. It is found in psychics and those who communicate with the spiritual world. These people can guide you to your path towards spiritual awareness.

An even deeper connection with spirituality is displayed through a white aura. This is the reflection of a person, who has comprehended their higher self and has flooded the world with enlightenment. White color is that of purity and people with white predominant color manifest cosmic wisdom. Green is the color of healing, peace and harmony. So these are also amazing properties, highlighted in your aura. Of course, as mentioned above, the aura is not static. On the contrary, it moves and changes constantly. Therefore, depending on your specific state at a time, it can show different colors. You should not worry about that, as it is perfectly understandable.

You can see the aura either of yourself, or of another person. In any case, you are going to need a dark background. If you are looking at another person's aura, you should allow a couple of minutes for them to get relaxed. At the same time, you need to let go of any thoughts and concentrate. Then, you should gaze at the person, but not straight at them. Try looking a little further away from their head. In this way, you maintain your perception of the person's presence, but without looking directly at them and identifying any details of their face, or shape.

It is important that you focus on the area of the head, as this is where you get the strongest energy fields. Be silent during the entire procedure, while you are trying to distinguish even the faintest impressions. In the beginning, you will be able to see a white line shaping the person's aura. This is just the first step. As you continue focusing on the person, you will have the opportunity to discern the dominant colors of their personality. Through practice, you can go further than that and see the entire chromatic spectrum of the aura. For those who have been practicing this for long, it is even possible to do so without a dark background.

In case you wish to see your own aura, you should concentrate on your palm. Use a dark background again, but this time keep your fingers spread apart. Look right between the thumb and the index. Do not look away, as you will lose your focus. After a while, you will start seeing that white glow shaped right adjacent to your palm. It will be as if you have dipped your hand in that shimmering light. The more you concentrate, the more you will be able to discern your aura. It takes practice and an open mind, so do not get discouraged.

15

CHAPTER 4: SUPERCHARGING YOUR VIBRATION, QUIETING THE MIND, & TOWERING ABOVE NEGATIVE FORCES

If you take a moment and think about it, there is a whole lot of empty space within an atom. This is where vibrations take place, shaping the world all around us. Without vibration, there could be no life. By raising your vibration to the maximum levels, you will achieve the highest level of aliveness in yourself. A heightened vibration can transmute the energy in yourself and your home. So how can you manage all that? Is it 100% in your hands, or do you depend on others?

Basically, you need to understand that your feelings and thoughts translate into different vibrations. Low vibrations stem from negative thoughts and emotions, such as anger, sadness, depression, fear and despair. On a brighter note, happiness and optimism, love and affection.... These are all elements that make your vibrations higher. Just to keep a perspective, a healthy human body ranges from 62 to 70 MHz. As soon as your vibrating frequency drops below that point of 62 MHz, your cells begin to mutate. They deform and bring chaos into your life.

Your vibration is not only affected by what you feel. A lot

FULL MOON RITUAL MASTERY

of other factors contribute to that frequency. Imagine the food that you eat. Did you know that they can be destructive to your efforts towards reaching a higher vibration? If you consume a lot of dead foods, such as meat and poultry, you need to be aware that their frequency does not exceed 5 MHz. This is why it is important that you limit your intake of meat and its derivatives. Especially heavily processed food items should be eliminated from your shopping list. You do not benefit nutritionally from such a diet, while your energy is heavily compromised too.

On the other hand, there are foods that actually promote your vibrational frequencies and make you feel better. Raw almonds vibrate at 50 MHz and leafy greens can go as high as 70 MHz. Opt for organic, raw and unprocessed foods and incorporate them into your diet. In this way, you will get all the nutrients your body needs, without having to resort to chemical supplements. Furthermore, your body will thrive by absorbing the nutrients of such pure foods. Digestion is completed much sooner and there is little residue for your organs to filter and process.

Another helpful tip would be to use essential oils. They skyrocket your vibration and enable you to reach new heights. For instance, rose vibrates at a frequency of 320 MHz. This is absolutely amazing. Their aromas can lift your spirit and change your mood, so make use of their great properties. Frankincense, lavender, and chamomile all work wonders for your emotional health. At the same time, you can use crystals to raise the frequency at which you are vibrating. They can help you clear out negative energy and purify your environment. There are many different crystals, focusing on different aspects of your life. So pick the ones you truly need for optimal results.

Moving forward, it is important to express gratitude for your blessings in life. This is another wonderful way to elevate your vibration, as it motivates you to be grateful and satisfied about what you have accomplished in your life. Sometimes we get so consumed by our concerns and the goals that we have set, that we forget to say *'thanks'* for the things we already have. Gratitude is closely associated with abundance and this is quite similar to positive thinking. Rather than drown yourself in negative thoughts, fears and anger, concentrate on thoughts that spark joy. Be kind and this will return to you.

Another way to raise your vibration is to spend more time with people that vibrate at elevated levels. You must have noticed that there are certain people, who just walk into a room and the whole place suddenly lights up. These individuals have been blessed with a brighter energy. Through the Law of Attraction, you will receive that positive energy they are emitting by being close to them. In addition, you should spend more time meditating. Through this invaluable experience, you get in touch with your inner self and gather your thoughts on what actually matters. You learn to appreciate the moment, be present and clear out all the noise that might bring you down. More than that, you practice deep breathing. This helps you destress and relax.

Water allows your body to maintain its bodily functions and stay healthy. However, it also enables energy to circulate. By detoxifying your body, you get rid of negative energy and cleanse yourself on various levels. Simply by upping your daily water intake, you will start feeling amazing. Next, work out in a way that makes you happy. Dance, move around and feel the benefits of energy overwhelming you. We have not been designed to sit all day in front of a screen, or lie down on our sofa binging on TV. Bring motion in your life.

Techniques to Raise Your Vibration

Besides changes you can make in your daily routine, like the ones that have been described above, there are also several techniques you can incorporate for optimum results. These techniques will help you reach a higher vibrational frequency, so as to manifest the things you want in life. They will allow you to reach your divine self and clear any negative thoughts.

Flutter Breath Technique

The flutter breath technique is a great option for you to try out, as it enables you to connect to your higher self. You need to sit comfortably, in an erect position. This means that your chakras should be aligned, creating a channel for energy to flow through without obstacles. Then place your palms on top of your thighs, always facing up to receive. Remember to keep the tips of your thumb and index connected, gently touching each other. Keep the other three fingers connected, too. This is important, as you don't want to let the energy go to waste.

Stand in that position and rest. As soon as you feel relaxed, you are ready to move forward with your breathing. Close your eyes and start inhaling and exhaling through the nose as fast as you can. The aim here is to reach four times a second, which might sound impossible. However, through constant practice, you can achieve that. Even though you may feel like you cannot do this anymore, it is essential that you keep on breathing like that for two to three minutes.

After these two or three minutes, you can breathe deeply and gently. Always keep focused on your third eye chakra. This will help you realize your energy. It will be high, but a bit chaotic at first. Continue breathing deeply, in and out. Eventually, you will become aware of the subtle difference of your higher vibration. Through this technique, you can also focus on your manifestations.

Morning Yoga

Yoga is always helpful to introduce you to your spiritual self. Find a cozy place, bathed with sunlight and get your morning Yoga ritual. Get a comfortable seating position, with your spine erect and straightened all the way up to your crown. This helps your energy flow gently. Your palms should be placed on top of your knees. Inhale through the nose, exhale through the mouth. Practice these deep breaths for a while.

After having relaxed adequately, you can place your right palm onto your heart and your left palm onto your stomach. This will enable you to reconnect with your body. Continue breathing deeply. Next, place both your palms in front of your chest, in a prayer position. In this way, you are ready to set your intention for the day. What are you planning to achieve today? What is your goal? Take your hands and place them all the way on top of your head. Join them for a brief moment and then take them down to the ground as you are twisting your body on either side.

At this point, you should be comfortable and relaxed. Next Yoga position: Take your right hand and stretch it above your head, so that it reaches as far left as possible. Your left hand should simply touch the ground. Do the same in the other direction, continuing to breathe deeply. After that, you can take your hands and bend the elbows, touching each other in front of your chest. Open up, getting your hands on either side of your body as if you were opening a window. Close the hands and repeat the same pattern.

Stretch your arms on top of the head, in front of you and at the back. Then you can change your position. Cat-cow pose is perfect for now. So place your knees and palms on the ground. Inhale while getting the cat position, arching the back. Round your back as you are exhaling, for the cow pose. Repeat for a few times and then continue with the downward dog position. Create a triangle with your body, shifting a heel at a time. Next, do the forward fold position. You are free to experiment with different movements, as long as you feel the energy flowing.

In order to relax and get completely grounded, you are greatly advised to wrap up your Yoga ritual with a child's pose. Get your knees touching the ground, as you take your arms and stretch them as far as possible to touch the ground in front of you. Your whole body is relaxed and you concentrate on your breathing. Let go completely and feel yourself melt into the ground below you. Close this session by following the same routine as you did in the beginning. Sit comfortably, get your spine straightened and feel the energy flow through your chakras.

Fire Breath Meditation

By following this technique, you benefit from the massive energy of fire in your life. It is best if you can be outdoors for this meditation, as this will allow you to enjoy nature. In addition, you can get your feet standing on the grass. Grass will enable the energy of nature to run through you. However, even indoors you can do that with great success. Get your socks off and stand comfortably. Stop thinking about anything, since you cannot opt for a higher vibrational frequency if you are distracting your mind.

Calm your mind, so that it remains peaceful. Ground your feet and focus on your breathing. As you are inhaling, do that with your palms facing up in front of your chest, slowly elevating with your inhale. Respectively, as you are exhaling, keep your palms facing down in front of your chest and slowly move them downwards. Keep your eyes closed for a state of deeper relaxation.

So what you do is visualize every breath you take. You breathe in and then you move your breath into your stomach. This is the core of your energy, which will help you disperse that energy all around you. By using your hands, push the energy as you are breathing, so that it reaches your stomach. As you are doing that, you will be feeling a tingling sensation all over your body. It can be your face, your arms, even your feet.

After completing a round of this breathing technique, you might be experiencing dizziness. This is absolutely understandable, as it shows you have accomplished to raise your vibration. Slow your breathing, concentrate on calmness and get back to the initial state you were in. The more you practice this meditation, the more you will be amazed at the impact it has on your physical and spiritual self.

Practice EFT

EFT Tapping is an alternative method of dealing with pain and distress in your body. It resembles acupuncture, since it focused on certain parts of your body that can promote healing from within. According to EFT, the source of disease is nothing more than an imbalance of energy within your body. As a result, you should restore that balance to improve your health.

Of course, there are specific parts of the body based on the meridian points that you should focus on. These parts include your chin and upper lip, the area below your eyes, the eyebrows, under your armpits and your chest. These very parts are pathways that release any energy blockages, allowing the energy to flow through your body without any obstacles (Anthony, 2017).

If you want to try this out, you can start with a simple EFT tapping session. Take your one palm and begin tapping on the external part of your other palm. I know that you will be feeling your vibration rising by the second, which is great. As you are doing that, repeat positive affirmations. For instance, you can say *"I choose to raise my vibration," "It is my choice to feel good," "I am ready to raise my vibrational frequency,"* or similar statements that complete the effectiveness of EFT tapping.

Then, continue tapping your forehead and the area on the side of your eye. This is going to be extremely rejuvenating. You can tap right between your eyebrows, where your third eye lies, under the eyebrows, right below your nose and on your chin. Keep on saying all those wonderful things you wish to achieve through your tapping session. Be focused and detailed, as you will be manifesting your intentions. The more focused and detailed you are, the better the results. Do not forget to tap the area on top of your head, as well as your neck, your chest and armpits. This will help your energy flow, releasing any barrier. Just a few minutes every day will make a difference.

Absorbing Negative Energy

Apart from the techniques that are meant to elevate your vibrational frequency, you should also focus on how to absorb any negative energy or stress from your aura. It goes without even saying that there is negative energy flowing around, blocking your growth, joy and prosperity. How can you deal with that? Do you just settle for the fact that there is good and bad in the world?

It is in your hands to shelter your home and clear any negative energy that has been piling up all this time. One great way to do so is by casting a saltwater spell. What you need is any kind of salt, along with a jar. Pour ¼ cup of salt into the jar and then take warm water and pour it right in for the salt to melt. As you are doing that, repeat your intention: *"I am doing this saltwater to clear out any negative energy from my home."* Take a spoon and stir well, so that the salt is completely dissolved.

When the water becomes transparent, it is ready. Of course, you need to have some label to put on the jar. Write down the date, so that you can keep track of your progress. Along with the date, you can also write down the purpose of your spell. Repeat your intentions throughout the process and be as specific as possible. *"I am making this saltwater to clear negativity from within my home, cast away all the fear that is surrounding us and be free,"* or something like that.

After a month, you will get the results from this spell. Any negative energy will have displayed as a band around the jar. The water will have evaporated and crystals will have been formed in the bottom. In this way, any negativity is absorbed by this spell, rather than disperse in your home. It is interesting to keep track of the formation of the crystals, in comparison with the way you feel. For instance, if you have just had a fight in your home, check out the jar the next day. You will be surprised by what you see.

16

CHAPTER 5: CASTING YOUR IMPENETRABLE FORCE FIELD OF DEFENSE

Protecting your energy is of the utmost importance, because otherwise your whole life will lack balance. You are surrounded by an electromagnetic field, which determines every aspect of your being. However, there are several threats omnipresent that require your utmost attention. Even when you least expect it, you can be attacked by those who wish to undermine you. Never should you let your guard down, unless you want to take that risk of having your energy compromised.

When you fall asleep, your consciousness slowly drifts away. This makes way for those who wish to harm you. The results can be disastrous, including restless sleep, bad dreams, experiencing collective fears, lack of rest and so many other negative things. If you are determined to safeguard your energy, you should do that 24/7. Sleeping is not an exception to that. So it is imperative that you plan your strategy holistically, leaving nothing uncovered.

One of the best methods to create an impenetrable force field of defense around you is to use psychic protection with gemstones, crystals and amulets. There are items that have so great powers, being able to absorb any negative vibe and protect you and your home. In addition, quite a few different techniques are available for you to enhance your aura and expand it even further. There are specific meditations, mantras, visualizations and rituals that aim at making you stronger, keeping you protected at all times.

At nighttime, prepare for a restful sleep. You can wear a moonstone necklace to keep you protected. Clear the energy within your bedroom often, never allowing stagnant energy to mess with your inner balance. Complete the day with positive affirmation, setting your intentions for a peaceful, serene night ahead. Use essential oils that can be soothing and allow you to calm down and get ready for bed.

Finally, learn how you can connect with the archangels' energy to cast protection over you. Archangels such as Michael and Uriel are ideal in your endeavors. Michael is your ally in battle, so you should call on him when you are in need to fight. Uriel will protect your spiritual self, safeguarding your divine insights and inspiration. Even though the archangels are always watching over you, protecting you from above, you can always seek help from them to ensure your protection is indeed bulletproof.

AURA FIELD EXPANSION TECHNIQUE

By learning how to expand your aura, you master the art of protecting yourself from any negativity. You need to find out how you can create a powerful energy field, which is going to protect you against negative people and anything that might compromise your well-being. Of course, this energy field is not perpetual. On the contrary, you should make sure to refuel that energy once every month. It is advisable to keep track of your aura field expansion sessions, so that you identify when it is time to strengthen your defense once more.

What you need to do is bend your knees and sit on your calves, with your back straightened. In this way, you will feel the stress and tension on your calves, your thighs and legs. The more you practice this seating position, the more comfortable it is going to feel. Get your palms on your lap, facing downwards. Take a deep breath and repeat until you feel relaxed. Allow yourself to relax in this position, balancing out your energies.

Focus on your breathing and make sure that you exhale more forcefully—this is called *"fire breathing."* You should feel yourself breathing out and visualize how your breath expands your aura from within. By doing so, you create your own reality. Slowly but steadily, you will feel your palms generating heat. You will feel your forehead ready to explode with energy.

As you are visualizing this energy, shape it as a protective shield all around you. Let it solidify and keep it even in every part of your body. After completing this process, sit comfortably and realize what has just happened. You will feel your head slightly heavier. There will be an expanded aura all around you, which you will not be able to describe in detail. However, you will feel the difference.

Protecting Yourself from the Evil Eye

The evil eye is very powerful, reflecting the negative energy of a person that is sent out your way. It can be cast on both adults and children. A child that has been suffering from the evil eye will become irritable and will not stop crying. In an adult, symptoms vary greatly and include fever, body aches, headaches and other flu-like signs. An overall feeling that you are unwell and you do not have the power to stop bad things from happening will surround you.

How do you know that you have been the victim of the evil eye? First of all, you will know. Things will start falling apart so quickly, often without any indication of what is about to happen next. You need to make sure that you are protected at all times, because of the severity of this phenomenon. It is much better to be safe, than sorry. Protection is much better than the cure, after all.

Wear your amulets or a talisman representing the evil eye. Be sure to find something that appeals to you, so that you have it always on you. This type of jewelry will absorb the power of the evil eye. After getting in contact with the evil eye, the amulet will break or fall apart. If it falls on the floor, never pick it up. Replace it as soon as possible, as you will most likely suffer from similar attacks in the future.

If you do not know the intention of a person complimenting you about something, analyze their words. If they are wishing you health, happiness, prosperity or good fortune, but they never refer to God blessing you with all that, then you should be vigilant. The best way to protect yourself is by rejecting their energy altogether: *"I reject any negative energy you send to me."*

Finally, a word of caution. Even though you should feel free to do exactly what you want in life, this doesn't mean that you should not be careful. By exposing your happiness and success to the world, you are inviting the evil eye. Unfortunately, evil is not uncommon. Do not expose things that can trigger jealousy, envy and anger to others. Keep those precious experiences to yourself and to those you hold dear to you.

Opening Your Spirit Channels

You know by now how important it is to maintain a healthy energy field within our body and all around us. If you are determined to make the most of your energy, you should open your spirit channels to let it flow through you. The first energy channel is under your feet. Picture it as a thick layer of white light, under your feet and possibly below the surface of the earth. Then, the next energy channel is located around your navel and solar plexus area. Moving forward, the next channel is your heart and above that is your throat. Your third eye is obviously another energy channel within your body. Finally, there is the crown center right on top of your head.

Start by sitting somewhere comfortably, without any distractions. Release the tensions and let go of your thoughts. You need to be present and appreciate the moment. Concentrate on each breath, keeping your body centered and fully relaxed. You should be aware of your presence. When you have established this connection, draw your attention to the first energy channel. Direct this pure white energy towards that center. For even better results, you can chant *'ohm,' 'amen'* or *'ah'* at the same time.

Slowly but steadily, move the energy towards your second energy channel. Focus on that part of your body, between the navel and solar plexus area. The white light has flooded that area. Continue chanting. Feel the vibrations, as a response to the sounds you are making. Visualize the energy like a flower opening up and move the energy to the next energy channel. Watch your heart as it gets filled with that pure light, before transferring the light even higher to your throat. Chant again, as the energy is moving up to the third eye and finally your crown.

By that time, the energy will have flown through you and will be placed right on top of your head. Disperse it into the universe, as you continue feeling relaxed and chanting. Take a deep breath and experience a unique openness. You can repeat this session daily and whenever you wish to increase your awareness of the physical and spiritual self.

Protecting Yourself from Negative Energy

This is a simple exercise to protect you from negative energy, which you can practice before bed. Focus on your heart energy center and take deep breaths. It is best that you place both your palms against your heart, as you are doing it. Fill your stomach when inhaling and exhale deeply. In this way, you will get yourself focused and aligned. Next, imagine a white light of energy all around your body. This is like a force field of pure white energy protecting you. Although it might sound simple, it works really well to create a protective shield for you.

Another thing you need to be aware of is that you can say *'no.'* Do not absorb negative energy, do not internalize it, do not get consumed by that. Simply prevent yourself from getting sucked into a vortex of negativity. Allow yourself to let go of things that do not serve your own needs. It is your right to build that wall and prevent others from penetrating it unless you are OK with that. Why would you let these negative thoughts creep into you, draining your energy and making you feel lethargic?

Along with rejecting toxic and negative thoughts, you have the ability to control what each thing means to you. For example, let's say that you have been laid off from work. This is definitely a stress factor, as it represents a huge change in your life. However, you have the chance to think of it as something that opens up a whole new world of possibilities. Maybe you have been stuck in that work far too long. Find the silver lining in this incident, so that you focus on that. It is in your hands to turn even the worst situations into great opportunities for future growth.

Moving on, there is nothing wrong with setting boundaries and creating distance from people around you. It is true that many people are looking for a shoulder to cry on, a person to turn to in times of need. Although this is noble, you cannot be that person 24/7 and expect to thrive in your own life. Since you have a lot more to give, it is only fair that you maintain some boundaries, being strict about what others can get from you. Otherwise, you will always be distracted and eventually lose your own identity.

Confrontations can become a great ally of yours, even if you have grown into avoiding them altogether. Well, I am not saying that you should anticipate arguments. There are times, though, when you need to talk to the person who has been dragging you down and explain to them how you are feeling. Do not be afraid of the repercussions. In fact, this can be part of your exit plan for them. If you are struggling to cope with a person's character, if you are in a toxic relationship at home or at the office, then you must deal with it. Do not shy away from the challenge. Talk it through and either resolve the issue at hand, or get out when you still can.

What about Psychic Vampires?

Psychic vampires are people who suck the energy from other people. They do so, because they do not believe in their own ability to achieve what they want in life. So the only way to get what they desire is to drain it from others. You should be aware that they are weak, helpless and lack a connection with their spiritual self. In fact, what they do to you is a direct consequence of their divine ignorance. Therefore, you should not characterize them as evil.

When you get around such people, you start thinking negative thoughts. As a result, you feel drained of your energy.

You cannot cope with the challenges and you deprive yourself of a healthy, happy life. Now, take a moment and think about why these people get into your life in the first place. Maybe you want to be the *"good guy,"* hence you choose to be surrounded by those who are in need of your help. The Law of Attraction works like that. So even though you may have thought of psychic vampires as your exact opposite, they are not.

That being said, you need to steer clear of them. They are deceptive, they do whatever it takes to draw attention to them, they cause guilt and they defend their position against you no matter what. They do not trust anyone and many of them are dissociative. Contrary to common belief, they too feel like they are being drained of their own energy. But most importantly, they will not be saved, regardless of your attempts to save them.

A trap you should not fall for is believing that you need to be protected by them. This will make you feel like a victim. Instead, you need to create a white bubble of light that elevates your vibration, preventing the psychic vampire from affecting you. Since you deprive them of their source of energy, they will most likely leave voluntarily and never look back. Become stronger, so that they do not feed off your weakness.

Crystals and Gemstones for Protection

Crystals are powerful elements that date back to ancient

times. Some of them are 1,000 years old and they have been charged with exceptional properties that go far beyond what you could have imagined. There are crystals that have been shaped from minerals, as well as precious stones and gemstones of various shapes and sizes. They come in a multitude of colors and some of them are utterly breathtaking. You can find tiny crystals and gigantic ones that you cannot even grab in your palm.

When it comes to spiritual healing and cleaning of the negative energy floating in a room, crystals are extremely helpful. Due to their composition and thanks to their old age, they are able to absorb a lot of the toxicity that is out there in the world. As a result, they can absorb the negative energy found in your home. No matter if this energy has been caused by entities, by items or by curses, crystals can remove that. It might take time and it may damage the crystals themselves. However, they will do what it takes for you to dispose of the negativity that has been dragging you down in your own personal haven.

- Black tourmaline: It protects your physical body and it is highly detoxifying. Since it works best locally, you are advised to keep it close to you at all times. This crystal has a great energy, which is not compromised through the process of absorbing negative energy from its surroundings. Black tourmaline is considered a stone of protection, purification and cleansing.
- Black obsidian: Technically, black obsidian is not a crystal. It is volcanic glass, created from the hot lava flowing out of the volcano. Can you imagine its power? Having been born through the elements of water, earth and fire, this is a truly powerful item to have for protection. It is incredibly

absorbent and protects you from emotional exhaustion. This is called the gemstone of truth, because it clears your thoughts and shows you your strengths.
- Indigo gabbro: Quartz, Feldspar and trace minerals create Indigo Gabbro, this astonishing crystal that is highly programmable and allows you to receive the energy you most need at a time. You get great protection against electromagnetic frequencies, as well as entities. Another wonderful property is that this crystal is able to transmute the energy it absorbs.
- Shungite: there are different types of shungite, all of which are composed of 99% carbon. Fullerenes are elements of carbon, which offer this stone its healing and protective properties. Besides absorbing negative energy, shungite is also able to absorb any detrimental energies found within your aura.
- Amethyst: Amethyst is spiritually uplifting and it is connected to the energy of the violet flame. By having amethyst at home, you help create an environment that is safe and spiritual. It helps you stay protected from spiritual harm and allows you to calm down, relax and destress. This stone absorbs negative energy and transmutes much of it.
- Lapis lazuli: Lapis lazuli is another wonderful stone, protective on a psychic level. If you are even suspicious of having been targeted by black magic, this is a powerful item to hold on to. It also promotes charity of mind, which is invaluable in cases of psychic attacks and negative thoughts sent your way.
- Smoky quartz: This crystal is extremely protective

against electromagnetic frequencies, entities and curses. It is highly absorbent and it is quite wide in the range of protection. When you are having trouble, or you find yourself in a painful situation, smoky quartz will help you recover.
- Pink halo: This is also known as Himalayan salt. It is an extremely powerful crystal, used for protection within your home and around it. As it purifies your environment and clears it from negativity, it can also be a great addition to your working environment.

As you can see, these powerful items can absorb negative energy and protect you from it. Your home is a better and safer place, because of them. However, over time they become less effective. This makes sense, as they absorb anything toxic. So you need to make sure that you clean them regularly, restoring their initial composition. You can cleanse crystals and gemstones through various techniques.

One of the easiest and most efficient techniques is to clean them with running water. It would be best for you to go outdoors, in search of running water. Still, even at home you can use tap water and let the crystals soak for at least a couple of minutes. Cleaning crystals and gemstones with sea salt is another option. Just add a tablespoon of sea salt to a glass of water. Place your crystals inside and leave them overnight. Of course, you can use dry salt and cover the stones with it. Again, leave overnight for complete cleansing. Finally, you can use a Tibetan singing bowl. If the crystals and gemstones are small enough to fit, then place them inside. Otherwise, you can get the Tibetan singing bowl on top of them to vibrate and cleanse.

When you notice that your stones are fading away, losing their initial power and effectiveness, then it is time to charge them. You can use the different phases of the moon, depending on your intention. For example, the new moon enhances your intention for growth. So clarify your purposes and charge the specific crystals of yours under the moonlight. Alternatively, you can use sunlight. Using eclipse energies is another way for you to charge your crystals, while you can also bury them into the ground for a specific amount of time. All these techniques restore your stones' former properties and allow you to enjoy their full potential.

For programming your stones, you need to hold them in your left hand and bathe yourself in sunlight. You can do that outdoors, or if you stand by a window. Then, you must repeat the following sentence: *"I dedicate this crystal to light and love,"* in order to express your desire to use it for something good. Next, visualize what you want to achieve through the use of the specific crystal. Once you have manifested your desire, say out loud: *"I dedicate this crystal to the purpose of..."* and complete the sentence with what you want. This is it! Your stone has been programmed to help you in your endeavors.

❧ 17 ❧

CHAPTER 6: BEAUTIFY YOUR HOME, BEAUTIFY YOUR EXISTENCE

Your home is meant to be your shelter. When you walk through the door of your home, you should feel protected, safe and comfortable. This is the one place you control fully, the place where no one judges you. At home, people spend their happiest and most relaxing moments of their life. So what happens when your home is filled with negative energy? Should you just move, or is there a way to get rid of that bad vibe and restore peace and balance?

Sometimes it can be hard even to detect negative energy at home. There are however warning signs that we simply cannot ignore. Toxic relationships bring out negativism in all its glory. When this negative energy circulates in your home, it will attract more negativity. Over time, the negative energy will pile up and you will feel suffocated under all that pressure. Along with that, when family members or flatmates place the blame on each other, this creates an imbalance of huge proportions. Negative energy blocks your view of acknowledging who is to blame, resuming responsibility when necessary.

Other signs of negative energy in your home feature non-stop complaining, as well as heavy criticism. In any way, you can always look at a glass as half-full, or as half-empty. When there is bad energy, you usually opt for the latter. This creates a vicious cycle, which you are struggling to get out of for your own good. Last but not least, a red flag about negative energy at home is clutter. When your home is packed with unnecessary belongings, along with countless piles of documents, unwanted things that you just can't decide to let go of, it makes sense the energy flow is disrupted.

You need to create a positive, high vibration environment. As a result, you will enjoy spending your time at home, whether with the people you love or alone. Beautify your home, in order to beautify your existence. In fact, archangels like Metatron and Uriel can beautify your home. Metatron assists you in clearing any blockage or negativity from your body or from your personal space. Uriel is the archangel of inspiration and ideas.

There are multiple different techniques enabling you to call on the archangels. You can use meditation, setting your intention to call on the archangel for protection. Focus on your breathing, by calming down your mind and directing your desire to connect with the archangel on a deeper level. Alternatively, you can use exercises, mantras and affirmations. When succeeding in establishing your connection to the divine, the archangel will activate your *"Ascension Pillar of Light."*

How to Detect and Clear Negative Energy

As discussed earlier, there are several warning signs that should tip you off about the presence of negative energy within your home. Nevertheless, if you are looking for some tangible evidence, then you can experiment with some common ingredients you can find in the kitchen. Through these simple experiments, you will see remarkable results that allow you to understand where there are blockages of energy.

The first thing you can do is get fresh lemons and place them in every room. Make sure that they are in plain view and leave them for a couple of days. After that, go back and check their exterior. What does it look like? If your home is free of negative energy, then you will notice that the lemon has not changed at all. In fact, you can rest assured that it will ripen naturally, after a long time has passed.

On the other hand, negative energy can be manifested through black dots or shades on the external surface of the lemon. The lemon will be withered or maybe it will have grown green. In severe cases, it may also be disfigured. If you notice these changes, then you know you should purify the specific room where you have placed the lemon. Otherwise, the negative energy will continue on poisoning the rest of the house.

Another option for you to consider is using a glass of plain water, along with a tablespoon of sea salt and a dash of white vinegar. This mixture is transparent. You should place the glass in a room and leave it for a few days, even simply overnight. If the water remains transparent, then your room has no negative energy. However, if there are stains or if the water has changed color, then you need to focus on clearing negative energy right away.

The Power of Smudging

Burning sage is also known as smudging. This is a powerful technique, which was introduced to the world in ancient times, from indigenous populations that connected to their divine self through specific ceremonial rituals. It has become very popular all over the world, thanks to its amazing benefits in purifying negative energy. Therefore, you can use different varieties of sage bundles available to buy quite easily.

White sage has been considered one of the best qualities for cleansing negative energy. However, in several parts of the world it has almost been extinct. Even if you cannot find white sage, you can use any type and get the same purifying results. It doesn't matter what variety you choose to use for your smudging ritual, as much as how you perform it and how meticulous you are while purifying the place.

What you need to proceed with smudging is a lighter or matches, a heat-proof bowl and a sage bundle. Place the bowl on a steady surface and light the sage bundle. As soon as it starts smoking, you can purify yourself first from toes to head. After doing that, you should go to every room clockwise and let the smoke purify the air. Let it burn out and enjoy a clean, negative-free energy in your space.

It is important to note that you need to blow the sage smoke everywhere, even in the drawers and the closets. This is where your clothes are stored. Even if you are worried that they will smell like sage, you need to remember that you are wearing them all the time. As a result, they have accumulated all the negative energy from people who are looking at you with malicious intent, people who are envious of your success, even complete strangers.

Make Your Own DIY Spray to Remove Negative Energy

Wouldn't it be great if you could make your own liquid to protect yourself from negative energy? Indeed, you could even use it to purify the negativity from within your home, at the office and any other place. Well, the truth is that there are quite a few recipes available for you to experiment with, in order to create something powerful, without any difficulty. This is a simple DIY recipe that you can make yourself, so as to have a powerful ally in your effort to remove negative energy from your home. It doesn't require any technical knowledge and it can be done pretty fast. Remember that this recipe has no preservatives or chemicals whatsoever, so you need to renew it often. These are the ingredients that you are going to need:

- Rose petals (from 4 roses)
- Sage (10 leaves)
- Water (2 liters)
- A pot to boil the water
- Spray bottles

BRING THE WATER TO A BOIL AND THEN REMOVE FROM THE heat. Next, add the rose petals and sage to the water. Place a lid on top and let it sit, until the water cools down completely. When you remove the lid, you should see the rose petals having turned light pink or white. This is an indication that the water has soaked up all their powerful properties. Use a strainer to remove the roses and sage, so that the water is easy to pour into the spray bottle.

This is an all-natural spray, which you can use wherever you want. In order to prolong its expiration date, you can store it in the fridge. The reason for using the specific ingredients is that both roses and sage hold high vibrational frequencies. Therefore, they are exceptionally effective in clearing out negative energy. At the same time, this spray enhances the vibration of your personal space, lifting your mood and promoting a higher vibration for you to attract.

The water can be charged with the power of mantras, so as to absorb energy and purify the environment. You can choose a mantra to chant, if you want to enhance the effectiveness of the water in your DIY spray. The mantra of Lord Shiva is perfect to clear out negative energy. Otherwise, you can place your fingers within the water and set your intention. Repeat an affirmation like the following, while keeping your fingers submerged into the water: *"I am purifying this water, so as to clear any negative energy."*

If you are determined to make the most of your cleansing spray, then it is also good that you charge it with the power of crystals. Black tourmaline, selenite, moonstone and rose quartz, amethyst and so much more can contribute to the strengthened effectiveness of your liquid defense. Experiment with the crystals and gemstones of your liking, mixing them up with mantras and affirmations for optimal results.

Which Incense to Use for Clearing Negative Energy?

In times of extreme stress, when things are looking tensed at home, it is important to create a friendly, welcoming environment. This is exactly the place where energy flows abundantly, without any obstacles getting in the way and forming stagnant negative energy blockages. Incense can be proven extremely helpful in promoting such a positive transformation in your personal space. You can use them on a daily basis, removing any negative energy from your safe haven.

- Camphor: Camphor is often used when you are sick. Thanks to its intense aroma, it opens up your sinuses and helps you breathe deeply. However, camphor is also great at clearing the air and enabling the energy to flow smoothly. It cleanses space, making the area around you friendly and welcoming. Moreover, camphor is quite healing.
- Benzoin: Benzoin is another amazing incense you can use, in order to purify your home. It features intense vanilla aromas, mixed with a wood-like scent. This can be used to remove any negative entities, alongside bad vibes and negative spirits. Apart from driving away negative forces, benzoin is also beneficial to mental clarity.

- Dragon's blood: Dragon's blood incense greatly resembles a perfume. Not only does it get rid of negative forces within your home, but it also attracts positive energy. So while getting rid of the things you do not want, you can also manifest the things that you desire. In addition to its healing properties and protective features against negative energy, this is an incense that safeguards love.
- Frankincense: Frankincense is another wonderful incense that you can use, since it offers protection from negative energy and purification. It also enables you to become more spiritually aware, while at the same time it lifts your spirit and improves your mood to a great extent. If you are interested in boosting your clairvoyance and stimulating your intuition, then frankincense can work wonders for you.
- Amber: Amber is an equally powerful incense for you to try out, in order to heal your body and clear out all negativity from your personal space. It also helps you gain mental clarity and releases any negative energy that has been piling up and remaining stagnant for long. Due to the fact that it can directly affect electromagnetic energy, in Greek amber is called electron.
- Rosemary: Rosemary is the perfect incense for you to use, in case you are just moving into a new home. This is the resin of new beginnings. If you want to change an old habit of yours or set out on a new venture, then you need to burn rosemary. At the same time, it purifies the space and provides a welcoming atmosphere.
- Sandalwood: Sandalwood can be used to promote grounding in your home. You need to stay

connected to the earth and its power. Along with clearing the room of any negative energy, sandalwood also offers a way to stay connected to the central source of energy.

Of course, you can use any of these three incense options or mix them together. Make sure that you stick to a daily ritual, where you burn incense to purify your home and lift your spirit.

Using Essential Oils to Clear Negative Energy at Home

Aromatherapy is a holistic treatment that uses the extracts of herbs and plants, in order to stimulate positive emotions and promote healing (Camille Noe Pagán, 2018). Essential oils are of paramount importance to aromatherapy, as they offer a wide variety of scents that trigger different results. You can use the essential oils with the help of a diffuser, or you can spray them on their own. You can also apply them to your skin, or use them in a relaxing sea salt bath. When you diffuse essential oils, close the doors and let them run for a few hours. They will cleanse the negative energy from your home and lift your spirit naturally.

Lemongrass is an amazing essential oil that you can use, in order to clear negative energy at home. It disperses negativity, prevents feelings of depression, despair and lethargy.

Lemongrass cleanses the space around you and offers great healing properties. More than that, it is interesting to point out that lemongrass essential oil cleanses any blockages from the third eye chakra. By letting go of the stagnant energy, you can move forward with mental clarity. You can combine it with sandalwood, which is the oil of sacred devotion.

Experiment with different essential oils, making sure that you create a majestic, positive atmosphere within your home. Do not underestimate the power of aromas, stimulating your senses and promoting your connection to the divine.

Pour Salt in Your Home

Salt has been part of our life since antiquity. People in ancient times realized the value of this special ingredient, which comes from the sea and accompanies us in everything we do. Its purifying properties are undeniable. Therefore, you can benefit from its powerful properties and safeguard your home.

You should use fine salt for protecting your personal shelter. Start from the main room, getting handfuls of salt and spraying them in every corner. You need to follow a clockwise course while doing so, leaving no corner of the house without salt. Of course, you can sweep the salt after a while.

By doing so, you get rid of the negative energy that has been stagnant within your home. You also purify and protect your personal space, as well as avoid visitors that you do not want. Finally, through this ritual you attract abundance, prosperity and serenity in your home. If you are afraid of the evil eye, then salt along with black pepper mixed together in a bowl can serve as repellent.

You can also wash the objects you feel have been charged with negative energy, using warm water and salt. This will help transmute the negative energy. It is also advisable that you use salt to remove any bad vibes from your body. Just place some salt on your sponge or loofah and rub the skin until you feel relaxed.

As you can see, salt can be used in a wide range of situations. Incorporate it into your daily routine and you will notice its remarkable benefits in your life.

How to Clear Negative Energy in Your Home Quickies

To wrap things up, here's a list with easy-to-follow, fast instructions on how to cleanse negative energy at home:

- Smudge with sage: Light it up and wait for a few seconds, until you start blowing. As you blow, smoke will come off and disperse into the atmosphere. Do that in every room for thorough cleansing.
- Burn sandalwood incense: Follow the same procedure as with the white sage, in a clockwise motion. Sandalwood helps you remain grounded, in addition to its healing and protective use.
- Burn Palo Santo wood: Palo Santo wood has a rich fragrance, a little bit of citrusy and with pine undertones. It is a great way to clear negative energy within your home.
- Use a Tibetan singing bowl or Tingsha bells: In this case, use the powerful sounds of those special items. Go to every room, in all four corners. The results are amazing, as you are aligning the energies and using the sound as a vibrational asset.
- Pink Himalayan salt: Sprinkle pure pink Himalayan salt in the corners of every room, with a focus on those you feel the negative energy piling up. Otherwise, you can place bowls with the salt and leave it there to absorb any negativity.
- Meditation music: Another way to purify your

home from negative thoughts and energies is to use meditation music. It is soothing and you can choose the vibrational frequencies of your own liking to maximize the benefits.
- Indian basil: Simply by planting Indian basil at home, you are going to get a boost of positive energy and protection. In general, plants are beneficial in your effort to steer clear from negative entities.
- Declutter: Make sure that you throw away anything you do not really need. Instead of hoarding, choose whatever sparks joy in your life and get rid of the rest. You will feel an immediate sense of relief, as soon as you get rid of the old junk that has been occupying valuable space in your home.
- Tidy up: Along with decluttering, you should tidy up your home and keep it clean. There are dead skin cells all over the place, along with dirt, hair and so many things that mess with your home's energy. Clean them out!
- Visualize: Visualization is a wonderful ally in your efforts to keep your home protected, away from any negative energy. Get in a meditative state and visualize a white light on top of your home.
- Use crystals: You already know the importance of crystals. Make sure that you place them strategically all around your home, so that they can purify the space and absorb any energy that gets clogged up in the corners.
- Ask your spiritual guides for help: You can ask your spiritual guides to help you clean your home from negative energy. Reach out to your dearly

departed and seek their assistance in this noble work.
- Spray with the DIY negative energy remover: Use the DIY solution that has been described above for cleaning your home from any negative energy. If you don't have it at hand, then use rose essential oil, because of its high vibrational frequency.
- Use lemons: Place three lemons into a bowl filled with water and let them sit there. If there is negativity in the room, lemons will absorb it and cleanse the place from bad vibes. At the same time, when you place lemons in a room that has been contaminated with negative energy, the lemons will get disfigured.
- Cinnamon sticks: Cinnamon is a great ingredient, not only for spicing up your food. You can burn a cinnamon stick to remove any negative energy from your home. Otherwise, you can find cinnamon incense and scented candles to buy.

This is it! Keep those ingredients readily available within your home, resorting to them whenever you feel that negative energy is clogged up indoors. You do not have to spend a lot of time preparing rituals and trying in vain. As long as your efforts are targeted and to the point, they will be successful. Experiment with their use, either on their own or in combination with each other. Incorporate these cleansing rituals and you will definitely feel the difference right away!

❦ 18 ❧

CHAPTER 7: THE WAR YOU ARE DESTINED TO WIN!

We all come into this world carrying our own baggage, whether we are able to accept that or not. We are all flawed, and somewhere in our family history there is at least one rotten apple that we would like to distance ourselves from. There will be diseases in all of us, hardships and things that we feel we cannot survive. Some of these ordeals might be considered as curses, or evil spirits haunting you non-stop. Some others might say they represent dark psychology, reflecting the ability of a wounded soul to manifest these hardships, as a source of punishment or revenge.

That being said, these bad things do not all stem from some evil cause without further investigation. You should first discover the root cause of your issues, before moving forward with encountering them for good. Remember that faith offers you so much, in terms of emotional balance and stability. It allows you to heal your body and soul, experiencing great comfort and deep psychological recovery. Therefore, you need to maintain your faith throughout your endeavors to remove any types of negative energies or entities.

Even the darkest shadows within yourself can be cast away, if you follow the instructions that you are given and do not forget to protect yourself. It makes sense that all people tend to bury those emotions and experiences that had made them sad in the past. These traumatic experiences must get out in the open, even though they may make us feel uncomfortable. This book is meant to provide a loving approach to dealing with these catastrophic emotions, experiences, traumas.

No matter what has happened in your life, both your current and your past lives, you are destined to win this fight. By learning how to cope with the challenges and go to battle against any negative entity, parasite or attachment, you will have all the tools you need to succeed. It doesn't matter if you have suffered from these negative manifestations all your life, or you just discovered the true meaning behind your unhappiness. Believe in yourself and read along, so as to come up with a strategy you can easily follow at home.

Banish Negative Entities, Parasites, Attachments, Curses and Ill Wishes Forever

There are spirits trapped between two worlds, unable to pass on. These are called earthbound spirits and they might haunt you, messing with the positive energy of your home. What you need to do is to help these spirits to go into the light, clearing your place from their negativity. If you are wondering if you fall into that category of having a spirit trapped in your own shelter, then there are several warning signs to tip you off. For example, you might be seeing windows opening out of the blue and mirrors smashing. You may be hearing noises in empty rooms, taps or lights switching on and off in your absence.

The most powerful tool in your effort to remove these

spirits from your home is sage. It is extremely effective, as its smoke is able to eliminate negative energies and pulls them out of your place. It has been scientifically proven that by burning sage around your body, you can kill 94% of airborne bacteria (Collins, 2016). This is a great herb, which purifies the atmosphere and enables you to feel positive about the place you live in. Spiritual-wise, it works wonders and assists you in various ways.

So what you need to do is get a bowl and fill it with sage, after breaking it into small pieces. Be careful not to use sage sticks. Use a lighter or match to set sage on fire, blowing continuously to create smoke. Go back and forth in every room, letting the smoke disperse all around. Do not forget to pass by every corner, the windows and doors. Open the closets and blow the sage smoke, then head to the staircase, the attic, everywhere. When you are done, fill the bowl with cold water and get out of the house, closing all windows and doors. After an hour or two, come back and open every window to let fresh air flood your home. Hopefully, the earth-bound spirits will be long gone.

Have you ever suffered from a physical parasite? Maybe you ate something and a parasite has crept inside you, causing side effects. Spiritual attachments are parasites of non-human nature, entities that do not want to leave this space. They might even be extraterrestrial implants. They do not want to proceed to what lies ahead, either because they feel guilty, or because they are afraid. Of course, they may have been atheists who do not believe in a higher power. Therefore, they are stuck here. Unfortunately, you are vulnerable to such entities in a number of different cases. You can be intoxicated, or you may have sexual intercourse with a person who has one of these attachments, or you might be in a truly emotional state.

Crystals can also help you in your endeavors to remove entities and negative energy from your home. An amethyst, a rose quartz, a smoky quartz and others should be placed on the window ledge or at a corner of your room. Clapping is another method that allows you to remove those negative spirits. Just clap your hands in every corner of your home, helping the stagnant energy get unclogged. In addition, you can place sea salt in a bowl and then on top of it you can add a coarse crystal. Let it sit overnight and then clean the crystal with pure water. This will help release the excess negative energy.

Last but not least, you can choose to use a powerful prayer to remove those negative spirits from your home. A prayer is your commune with God, with the higher power. You need to remain in deliverance, in order to communicate with that high power and seek help to get rid of those entities. Call on what you believe, praising the Lord and expressing your gratitude: *"God, you are the beginning and the end, you are the alpha and the omega, you are the omnipresent light. You are my creator. I worship you, I thank you for my life. I pray for you God, all mighty. Please my Lord, raise the spirit of my dear brother and sister. Raise their spirit to another level. I pray that with all my heart."*

In this way, you will find that your genuine communication with the higher power has made these spirits go away. Of course, you can use your own words in your prayers. In fact, you can speak right from your heart. Say what you want to express in your own words, reflecting the way you feel about your creator, the creator of all things.

Past Life Cleansing

We have all lived in the past, but most of us cannot remember. Why does that happen? First of all, it is our limited perspective of a 3-dimensional world that prevents us from seeing the wider picture. Then, it is divine mercy that stops us from remembering everything in detail. After all, it is highly likely that in our past lives we have done some terrible things. So we are armored with a veil of forgetfulness, which lets us start over fresh. Finally, it is our conscience that has encompassed the best of our past lives and guides us to act based on love.

Can someone remember their past lives? Of course they do! It is important to remain calm throughout the process, sitting somewhere comfortable with closed curtains and dimmed lights. Steer clear from any electronic devices, including your phone. Avoid any distractions, hence choose a time of day when you have already relaxed from the echoes of your busy lifestyle. Use white noise or other soothing sounds, waves or waterfalls.

Now lay down with your back, get your arms on both sides and visualize a white light surrounding you. Concentrate on all your body parts, feeling the light protecting them with its pure, powerful presence. Repeat positive affirmations about the white light, such as: *"I am breathing in the powerful energy, I am protected by it."* Imagine your aura changing colors, as it expands.

You are ready to begin your journey. Picture a long corridor, with a door at its end. Observe every detail. Keep this in mind, as you will be able to come back again to do the same journey in the future. When you open the door, experience what you find. Feel the energy, listen to the sounds, notice the smells, the textures, anything you can recall. When you are ready to return, push the door gently. Receive that memory of your past life without judgment. Use it as a reference and be grateful for the experience.

By using your birthday, you can see your soul's characteristics based on your past lives. First remember the number of your birth month. For instance, May is 5. However, if you were born in November, then you will add the digits of 11 and get 2. Remember that number. Then, move forward with the day you were born. Again, if you were born on the 2nd day, you will keep it as is. Otherwise, you will add the numbers to get a single digit. Next, add the sum of the numbers composing the year you were born. For instance, 1966 should be 1+9+6+6=22. Finally, add your birth month, birth day and birth year numbers. If you ended up with anything ranging from 1 to 9, 11 or 22, this is your result.

- #1 Alpha: You are independent, concentrated on your goals and rebellious. You do not feel the need to please others, as you are perfectly fine relying on your own strength.
- #2 Peacemaker: You are part of a team, supportive with ambitions to evolve and expand your knowledge. That being said, you are not at all selfish, but take into consideration the common good.
- #3 Creative: You are an influencer, inspiring others through your positive look at things to follow your lead and become more optimistic in life.

- #4 Practical: You are honest, just and reliable. Your practical spirit helps you in everyday life, as you find solutions to problems and help others see more clearly.
- #5 Free spirit: What drives you is freedom, adventure and the will to explore new uncharted territories. Your mind never ceases to dream big.
- #6 Compassionate: You protect others and love humanity. A compassionate person deeply cares about the world, protecting mankind and caring for the future.
- #7 Truth seeker: In constant pursuit of the mysteries of the world, the truth seeker exposes the lies and focuses on cross-checking evidence.
- #8 Leader: You are successful and you want to drive others to glory. You are always ready to fight for what you believe is right alongside your companions.
- #9 Socially conscious: You are ready to sacrifice yourself for the common good, since it is society that you are interested in protecting more than anything else.
- #11 Karmic master: Artistic, intuitive, with a higher sense of consciousness, the Karmic master develops a keen eye for detail, delving into the mysteries of life.
- #22 Master builder: Strong-minded, you influence others and unite them under a common purpose. You are a divine presence on this earth.

Having lived so many lives, sometimes we drag bad karma that affects us dearly in our current state of life. By clearing your past lives' karma, you get to relieve yourself from all the things that have been keeping you away from your goals.

Karma can affect you in many ways. For example, you may be struggling to lose weight in vain. This can be because in your past life you had been starving. As a result, this pattern is affecting your healing and growth in this lifetime.

In order to clear past life karma, we need to be fully committed to our current life goals. We must be mindful of our vibrational frequencies at all times. Where do you consume your energy? Do you make good use of that, pursuing your dreams? Or are your thoughts chaotic, not serving your purpose at all? You need to be strict with yourself, if you want to engage in past life clearing. You have your own life to live right now, rather than contemplating the complexes and problematic situations emerging from the past.

Go against your normal programming. It doesn't matter if you have been taught that as you were growing up. If it's not serving your needs and goals, then you need to reprogram yourself. Consciously choose new thoughts, new beliefs, new feelings of optimism and happiness. Along with that, it is imperative that you express your emotions as soon as you realize them. In this way, you can vent and get it off your system.

The reason for doing that is to allow yourself to grieve. You have never been given this opportunity, so you should embrace it, before getting rid of your prior dysfunctional behavior. EFT tapping can help you out with that, as well as keeping a journal or saying a prayer out loud. Finally, you can do a contract release with the behavior that does not serve you. Visualize cutting the cord of anything you wish to change in your life. Write down this contract or say it out loud.

CHAPTER 8: CLEANSE YOUR OWN ENERGETIC FIELD TO SKYROCKET YOUR JOY

I am sure you are looking forward to cleansing your energetic field. This is essential, if you want to experience a happy and prosperous life. There are energy centers in our body, defining our health and the way we feel. These energy centers are strategically located along our spine, creating a virtual column of energy flow from the ground to the sky above. They reflect the deeper and uninterrupted connection between the earth and the universe. It is eternal and omnipresent. If you want to align fully with the cosmic energy, then you need to make sure you become a vessel of energy yourself.

However, on several occasions this energy flow is disrupted violently due to various reasons. Sometimes a disease strikes, causing imbalances from within. Stress and anxiety, fear of the unknown, feelings of self-doubt and helplessness only add to this phenomenon of clogged energy centers that do not quite serve their noble purpose. They get cluttered, unable to permit the energy flow that is of the essence for your very existence. It is in your hands to take charge and restore your energetic balance as soon as possible.

In the Orient, energy centers have been named *'chakras.'* Below, you will see how to cleanse those chakras and boost their functionality. Each of these energy centers has been focused on a specific organ of the body, which means that even the slightest lack of balance will have a direct effect on your physical health state. It is like a valuable cog in a wheel. Without it, the wheel will not move and this will be disastrous to the entire mechanical structure.

Although typically these are the seven chakras, you should also concentrate on another organ of your body. The thymus gland is located right below your throat chakra, sticking out in the middle of your chest. By activating the thymus, you enhance your immune system and skyrocket your energy. If you want to activate this gland, you need to close your eyes and visualize that it opens up gently and utterly. Imagine a flower blossoming, with each petal slowly opening up and revealing the impressive interior. The flower is pink and it expands through each motion. It becomes wider and goes further with each breath you take.

By default, your thymus gland begins shrinking in size at the age of 16 and it continues shrinking with age (M, 2019). You can reverse that phenomenon with the power of your mind, or at least delay it from happening. By visualizing this expansion of your thymus gland, you will most likely start feeling it vibrating more heavily. It will be pulsing. Over time, this gland will allow you to reach higher levels of divine spirituality. You will be more receptive to initiations, while comprehending your uniqueness and putting it to use.

Now that you have activated your thymus gland, let's move forward with a chakra cleansing session that assists you to flood your body with pure energy. Be meticulous while performing this cleansing, as you will need to get rid of every single hint of negativity from your body.

Chakra Cleansing

As you know, there are seven chakras in your body. These represent your energy centers, where the energy flows smoothly and allows your body to thrive. In order for you to maintain optimal health and balance between the body, the mind and the psyche, you should make sure that your chakras are clean. They should be free from any distractions or clogging that might jeopardize smooth and uninterrupted flow of energy. Therefore, it is important that you proceed with a ritual, allowing these chakras to be kept open at all times. You can do it in the morning or set a reminder on your calendar to perform this ritual weekly.

Starting from the top, we find the Crown chakra. It is located on top of your head and reflects your ability to connect to the spiritual world. Right between your eyebrows, there is the next chakra—the Third Eye chakra. This is directly associated with your intuition and your spiritual powers. Next, there is the Throat chakra. It is responsible for your ability to communicate with others and express yourself. Your Heart chakra is obviously connected with love, appreciation and affection.

Moving on, we find the Solar Plexus chakra below our chest. This is the chakra related to our sense of self-worth and confidence. Sacral chakra is located below your belly and is connected to your sexuality. It offers you a feeling of abundance and pleasure. Finally, there is the Root chakra. This is where it all starts. This chakra is connected to our grounding experience, representing our foundations in life.

How can you cleanse your chakras? One thing that you should do is get a smoky quartz crystal and hold it in your left hand. This is your receiving hand. Then what you do is place the crystal on each chakra, repeating positive affirmations relevant to the specific energy center.

- Begin with the Crown chakra, placing the crystal

on top of your head as you repeat the following: *"I am aware that I receive the wisdom I request always"*
- Continue with the Third Eye chakra, repeating affirmations like this one: *"I understand that my intuition is the way God communicates with me and allows me to see clearly"*
- Then, place the crystal on your neck to cleanse your Throat chakra, repeating: *"I communicate effortlessly and genuinely with everyone around me"*
- Move on to the Heart chakra, keeping your eyes closed and saying the following: *"I am Love, I deserve to love and be loved unconditionally and utterly"*
- When you move further down to your Solar Plexus chakra, you should say affirmations like this one: *"I always have the power and drive to succeed in the goals that I set in life"*
- Now that you have reached the Sacral chakra, you should focus your affirmation on your sexuality: *"I feel desire, pleasure, sexuality and self-confidence"*
- As you have made it to the Root chakra, complete your affirmations like that: *"I am abundant in energy and strength. I express my unique self in the perfect manner"*

Practice Self-Healing through Qi Gong

Qi Gong is an ancient traditional technique from the Orient, combining deep breathing, along with specific movements and meditation for achieving optimal results in your inner balance. Your body has the ability to heal itself from within and Qi Gong opts at promoting such properties. Below, you will find a simple yet highly effective routine to energize your body, cleansing your energetic field and casting away all negativity.

Stand up comfortably and open your hands with bent

FULL MOON RITUAL MASTERY

elbows, just like you would open the window shutters at home. Inhale through the nose. As you exhale through the mouth, curl your back and face towards the ground, with your elbows almost touching each other. In this way, you loosen your spine and create a pillar of energy. Repeat 8 to 10 times and then relax your hands. Now, take your palms facing up and shake your wrists. This exciting movement opens the energy pathways that go all the way to your palms, communicating with your heart meridian. As you are doing that, take deep breaths inhaling from the nose, exhaling from the mouth.

After repeating for a whole minute or two, you will feel a tingling sensation. You are ignited with energy. Next, you need to connect to the earth. Shift your weight towards the heels and experience gravity. Let your body get into full alignment with the gravitational power, so that the earth charges you with its powerful energy. Do not forget to keep your palms facing down. Move them up and down, as you are trying to control that energy. Next, take your right palm and place it in front of your belly facing up, while the left palm is on top and facing down. You should feel the energy between your palms. Slowly move your left palm towards your forehead, so that you create a connection between your mind and the body.

What you do after that is to lower your left palm steadily, in order to reach all your energy centers. You should establish energy connections between your mind and your throat, your heart, your solar plexus and below that until you reach a point where your two palms almost touch each other. Then, rotate your palms and move them further apart and close together. This allows you to control your energy completely. Now that you have charged your hands with this vast amount of energy, you can channel it in the parts of your body you feel most vulnerable. You can channel it to the back of your neck, on your chest or anywhere else you want to soothe.

A Morning Ritual to Cleanse Your Aura

Do you want to start your day energized, ready to take on any challenge that comes your way? Then it is imperative that you clean your aura, so that you restore your body's balance and enjoy its powerful properties. Each morning you should get up and start your day with a tall glass of water, infused with mint leaves. You can also use cucumber slices, fruit or other herbs and spices to mix it up. You will hydrate your body and detoxify from any negativity. Open the windows, so as to flood the room with sunlight and get fresh air. The energy of the sun is impeccable.

Turn on high vibrational music that uplifts your spirit, in order to complement your morning ritual. Take Palo Santo wood, so as to perform a purification of natural cleansing energy. Burn it all around your room, while thinking happy and positive thoughts. As soon as you are down, you will feel so rejuvenated by the exciting aroma it gives off. If you have a salt lamp, then you can turn it on to add to the positive energy within your room.

Then, close your eyes and meditate. Focus on the uplifting spiritual music, the soothing sounds and the intoxicating aromas. Say what you are thankful for in your life. By expressing gratitude, you instantly increase your vibrational frequency. After completing your meditation, it is time to fully cleanse your aura. Get into your shower and let that pure water run all over your body. This is a highly therapeutic experience, allowing you to fully relax. If you have time, taking a bath with Epsom salt is great for the purification of your aura. If you don't, however, you can use dead sea salt. This is a type of salt that has magnesium and a lot of other minerals, benefiting your skin by removing dead cells.

Finish your morning ritual by writing down your positive affirmation in a journal and set out for a new, wonderful day filled with energy!

Energy Cleansing Using Salt

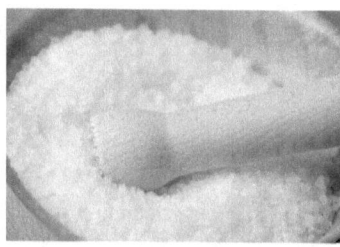

Salt is a mineral and a natural cleanser. People cannot even begin to imagine what their life would be like without the presence of salt. It is always there on our table, when we share our food and we want to make it tasty. It also accompanies us in summer vacations, when we dive into the crystalline waters of the sea and taste its presence on our skins and our lips.

Besides all the important benefits of salt, it is also used for spiritual purposes. It is one of the purest forms of protection for your home, yourself and any other place you wish to safeguard from malicious entities. You can cleanse your home using a homemade solution made with water, baking soda and salt. This will not mess with your home's energy and balance.

However, you can use salt directly to eliminate negative energy with its power, through a simple yet effective technique based on Feng Shui.

Get ¾ cup of coarse salt. Then, place 6 I Ching brass coins and place them inside the salt, in a circular shape. After that, get purified water and pour it on top of the salt. You do not need to use a lot of water, just a couple of inches above the salt surface. Place the container somewhere you can easily notice daily. As the days pass by, you will see a large crystal shaping. The water will react with the salt and the brass, creating an impressive crystal that will eventually overflow. According to tradition, this crystal absorbs any negative energy. At the same time, it serves as an excellent visual stimulant of the removal of negativity from your home or yourself.

Egg Healing

Are you experiencing a period of great stress? Are you having nightmares? There are moments when you feel uncertain or you are seeking a deep cleansing in your home. This is when you should turn to the subtle yet powerful properties of the egg. Even if you are skeptical as to whether or not it is going to work, you have nothing to lose. In fact, you will be amazed at the results.

Close your eyes and take deep breaths to relax. Move the egg around the head and rub it over the eyes, behind the ears, at the back of the scalp and down the chin. Then, roll the egg in front of your chest. Swirl it and then move it across each arm, on top of your shoulder and all the way down your palms. Pay close attention to that, as your arms represent an important energy center. As you are passing the egg through each finger, you can hold it within your palm for a few moments. Make sure that you then rub the egg again on your chest, across your angel wings and along your spine.

Move forward with your legs, focusing on your kneecaps,

your feet and ankles. Get the egg through each toe and then move it on the soles of the feet. Finally, blow on the egg three times. This will allow you to release your inner tension. During the egg healing ritual, you should be careful not to break the egg. However, you need to be prepared for the fact that the egg can weigh a lot heavier than before, due to the accumulated negative energy. This is why sometimes the egg might even explode.

Another option for you is to use 2 eggs, 1 white candle, a glass of water and some sea salt. First of all, light the white candle and let it burn out on its own. Then, start cleansing your body with the help of the egg. While you are doing this, you should praise the Lord and be thankful for your blessings in life. Ask that all the evil spirits and negativity are absorbed by the egg. Once you are done, you should take the egg and break it inside the glass of water. This will show you what is wrong.

If the yolk gets to the bottom of the glass, then you can sigh with relief. On the other hand, if it stays in the middle or floats on the surface, it means that evil powers are affecting you. If there are a lot of bubbles all around the yolk, then this is the negative energy that makes you feel exhausted and lethargic. In case a figure is displayed on the glass, this is the object of your concern. If there are pointy edges on the surface of the glass-like needles, they represent the negative entities undermining your well-being.

Maybe you see a coat surrounding the egg yolk. This means that there is someone constantly casting negative energy on you. If you notice red or black spots on the yolk, it means that you will encounter disease in your life. A cloudy yolk usually means that you have been the victim of the evil eye. Once you have finished observing the yolk, add sea salt and flush it down the toilet.

CHAPTER 9: WHAT IS WITHIN, WILL BECOME A REALITY ON THE OUTSIDE. MAKE WHAT IS WITHIN BEAUTIFUL

In this section of the book, you are ready to create a new reality from within you, so that you can project it to the world. There are techniques such as EFT tapping, TRE, mantras, meditation and so much more that can help you change your world. You need to disconnect from the ego to clear space, so that negative energy cannot be self-created and pollute the world. Clearing old conditioning that creates negative energy is of paramount importance, if you want to affect the universe in a positive manner.

There is a whole new world before your eyes and you have the power to shape it exactly like you want, instilled with the qualities of your higher self. This world will be loving and accepting. It will not be poisoned by the negativity drawn from selfishness, revenge, envy and jealousy. Instead, it will promote happiness for every being on this earth. You have the power to achieve all that, if you simply manifest what lies within your soul. Make it beautiful, so that the world can see your masterpiece. There are no limitations as to how to shape your reality. Use your imagination and do exactly what you want to do, making sure that the end result is aligned with the cosmos. Find out how to best express yourself, by creating the world around you in a way that makes you happy. This is going to be a fascinating journey.

Use the tools that appeal to you the most, in order to shape your inner self in a way that inspires others to follow your lead. The techniques shared below are self-applied, meaning that you can do them on your own. They are easy to follow, introducing you to different holistic approaches of energy healing. EFT tapping is based on the belief that your energy is soothed and redirected through tapping on acupressure points around your body. These are the meridian points, including many different spots around your head, on your crown, under the armpits, in front of your chest and on the exterior of your palms.

On the other hand, TRE is an easy tool for you to release trapped trauma and energy from within your body. This technique can be used to bring your nervous system back to a steady balance, making space for you to achieve higher vibrational frequencies. You already know how important it can be for you to do so, since all negativity is related to low vibration. By finding a way to get around this, you effectively deal with the phenomenon of attracting negative situations in your life.

EFT Tapping for Clearing Negativity

Have you ever considered making the world a better place through your own actions? EFT tapping can help you with that, energizing those parts of your body that clear negativity and promote happiness. You should take full responsibility for your own joy, with the active contribution of tapping sessions. What you can do is start tapping the external part of your palm, while repeating positive affirmations that cast the world's negativity aside. You can continue tapping several spots on your face (the area under your eyes and on their side, your third eye, your upper lip and chin, your cheekbones and forehead). Below you will find a typical script of clearing negativity within the world:

"Even though there is negativity in the world, I choose to be happy and positive. I accept myself completely, I love and honor myself. Although at times I encounter negativity, I choose not to spread it in the world around me. My choice is to spread happiness instead. I give myself permission to be happy, even though there is evil and negativity in the world. It doesn't affect me. Negative people don't affect me. I will affect them, making them dispose of their own negativity, spreading happiness even wider. Although I get exposed to negative vibes, I choose not to spread them. I clear that out with help from others and continue being happy. I share love, affection, joy and positivity to the world."

There are moments in your life when you feel consumed by energy vampires. EFT tapping can help you deal with this negative experience, if you adjust your script accordingly. As you are moving your fingers through the various meridian points all around your head and body, repeat something like that: "I love and honor myself, even though there are vampires sucking the energy from my body. It is my choice not to let them drain me of my energy, I continue to love and accept myself. Although these people get in the way and prevent me from doing the things I want in my life, I deeply accept and love myself. My intention is to show these energy vampires the way to live without absorbing my energy and bringing me down. I have to put up with them, although they make me feel powerless. My choice is to reclaim my energy and the power that I possess, so as to stop being the victim in this situation."

Another approach would be to use the energy EFT protocol, while invoking angelic power and protection. Your feet should be touching the ground, ensuring that you have higher energy flowing through you. To help you with your session, you can call on the archangels of your choosing. You can call on archangel Michael, archangel Zadkiel and your own guardian angel. Place both your palms in front of your chest, right in the center of your heart. Take deep breaths, so as to maintain your serenity and inner balance.

Once you feel totally relaxed and in sync with your energy, place your right palm on different parts of your head. Start with your Crown chakra and move further down to the forehead, the third eye, the area below your eyes and all the spots you would normally be tapping in a typical EFT session, repeating the following: *"I am releasing negativity now from my body. Thank you angels for enabling me to do that. I don't need to hold on to that toxic energy, so I am letting it go."* After that, touch your left fingers with your right palm and repeat how pure and revitalized this energy feels.

When you finish, you can start over with a different script that enhances your intentions. *"Thank you for the violet flame energy that runs through me. I am grateful for the pure violet energy within me and around me."* To conclude your EFT tapping session, you should place both your palms against your chest. This was your starting position. Close your eyes and visualize the archangels embracing you and offering their protection through the violet flame.

Shamanic tapping is another option for you to clear your mind from all negativity. In this case, again you move your fingers to various parts of your head and body, tapping them gently. You should stand in front of a mirror throughout this session. To elevate your vibration and remove negative thoughts, you can ask for forgiveness about anything bad you have done. There is nothing wrong with assuming responsibility for your actions. In fact, it shows that you understand what is right and wrong, what is good and bad. So you can repeat the following affirmation: *"I am sorry. Please forgive me. I love you."*

After completing this tapping session, you should get your

palms in front of your chest and start rubbing them. As you do, begin setting them apart slowly and continue the same motion. In this way, you will be able to generate energy and transfer it from your palms. You should set your palms apart gradually, increasing the distance between them slowly. When they have enough distance apart, you can rotate them so that you form a ball of energy. As soon as the energy is accumulated, you are free to place it on top of your head. It will be like bathing yourself in pure energy. Pull this energy down with both your palms, redirecting it all over your body and repeating how grateful you are for what you have received.

TRE to Release Past Trauma

TRE are exercises used to destress and remove past trauma from patients. They focus on tremors of the muscles, in order to release the tension formulated in the body. Once you put too much pressure on a specific muscle, you get a natural reflex. This is the tremor, which is beneficial to restore the balance from within. As a result, your nervous system calms down. It is a perfectly safe and greatly efficient technique, composing of various innovative exercises that are simple to execute. However, it is advisable that you remain within a controlled environment at all times. Otherwise, your reflexes might cause discomfort.

It can be seen as a combination of yoga, health counseling and massage treatment, when it comes to the provided benefits. If you want to try TRE out to clear out negative energy from your body and surroundings, you need to pick a comfortable place to lay on. You can use a yoga mat or a soft rug. Your intention is to help your body reach a point where it is almost exhausted. To do so, you can lean against a wall with your knees bent. Imagine that you are trying to sit down on a virtual chair right below you. Slide with your back as low as you can, while maintaining strength over your legs. When you feel like you have reached a point where you are trying too much to hold on, then stay in this position. Lift your heels for optimal results.

After a few seconds, you will feel your muscles burn. Stay in the very same position, until you cannot take it anymore. Then, what you do is lift your weight and move your torso a bit higher. It is like you are trying to sit on a slightly taller chair. You do the same, until you feel your legs slightly shaking. This is when you know you have activated your muscles through TRE. If you lay down on the mat, you will experience the tremoring that releases tension and clears the energy.

Another option for you is to fold your body and stretch, trying to reach your toes with your hands. This is equally challenging for most people, as your muscles are under pressure and you are trying to maintain your balance. Alternatively, you can start by laying down on the yoga mat. Your back is on the ground and your legs are bent before you, with your feet touching the ground. What you do is spread your legs and try to make your feet touch one another. It seems like a frog position. Once you are comfortable doing that, you can begin spreading your inner thighs even further and lift your hips.

TRE can assist you in reducing the tension and anxiety, lifting your spirit and creating a welcoming environment. Your vibrational frequencies get higher, thanks to the reflexes that make you shake. In addition, TRE helps you in dealing with chronic pain and promotes emotional resilience.

Instant Aura Cleansing

Your aura is meant to protect you at all times. Nevertheless, there are moments when it becomes so cloudy or foggy that you need to cleanse it. If you don't, it will not perform its best and consequently lead to spiritual imbalances manifested into your life. Instant aura cleansing is quite simple and easy to complete on your own, even though supervision is required for those of you who are new to this spiritual experience.

What you can do is stand up comfortably and close your eyes. Visualize that your heart is opening up like a flower blooming. Request that you are bathed in divine light and love, calling on your archangels and spiritual guides. Ask that your aura is thoroughly cleansed, shielding your powerful energy. After finishing with your requests, visualize a pure golden light from the divine right on top of your head. This is the source of light shining bright above you, having traveled through the Great Central Sun into our own dimensions and existence.

The light will slowly come down on you, following the shape of your body and filling you with divine energy. Feel this light going through your entire body, from head to toes. It will then be absorbed by the ground, shaping a platform of light below you. A second golden orb of light will then come and lower itself, bathing you once more with its divine nature. This time, it will remain in your abdominal area. Visualize that it stays there, as you are breathing in and expanding it with every breath. Your vibration is elevated, as this light is purifying your aura and balancing your spirit.

A third light moves towards your Heart chakra, where it rests and fills your heart with pure bright light. The light is illuminating your aura, expanding in every direction. Once again, another golden orb of light is concentrated around your head and illuminates your third eye. These three distinct energy centers that have been formed in your abdomen, your heart and your mind are perfectly aligned with the deep energy center of the earth's core, as well as the ultimate energy source of the Great Central Sun. This creates a steady pillar of energy flowing through you, cleansing your aura and removing anything toxic.

You can repeat the same visualization as frequently as you like. It will always help you to get grounded and attune to your divine nature. As you become more familiar with the spiritual world, you will be able to achieve even greater connection, activating your energy centers and allowing yourself to shine.

CHAPTER 10: AMAZING GUIDED MEDITATIONS TO BANISH NEGATIVE ENTITIES, CLEANSE YOUR AURA AND SUPERCHARGE YOUR LIFE

By now, you are well aware of the amazing benefits deriving from clearing any negative energy from your body and your home. Now you are ready to continue with guided meditation, in order to experience the wonderful results. Get in a receptive state, ask for help from your spiritual guides and be prepared for the gorgeous changes lying ahead. Through these easy-to-follow guided meditations, you will be able to channel your energy and request the things you seek most in your life. Do you want to clear the atmosphere in your home or at the office? Do you wish to confront a traumatic experience from a past life that has caused you to get stuck in an endless loop?

You have the power to request help from the archangels, reaching out to your divine spirit. They are here to protect you, offering their support and guiding you through the most difficult times. Whether you want to banish an evil spirit, motivate an earthbound entity to pass on to another space, attract abundance or cleanse your electromagnetic field, meditations are a powerful ally of yours. They help you concentrate on your intentions, express them firmly and with absolute clarity.

Below you will see 5 different guided meditations for you to try out. Some of them are simple, whereas others require the presence of the angels to guide you. Depending on your needs and desires, you can choose the meditation that ticks all the boxes for you, allowing you to shine.

Home Protection Meditation with Crystals

This guided meditation will help you protect your home from any negative entities, purify the atmosphere and attract positivity, feeling safe and secure. It will allow you to get rid of unwanted energies that mess with your balance, restoring your inner peace and serenity. For this meditation, you are going to need 4 white candles, 4 black gemstones (black tourmaline, black obsidian and onyx) and eight clear quartz crystals. You can omit the last part, although it amplifies the benefits you get out of the entire protective session. If you want, you can burn sage for a complete reset of your energies.

Place one candle in front of you, one at the back and one on each side of yours. Light the candles and place the black gemstones in between them. If you also have the crystals, you can place each one by the candles and the gemstones. Light the sage and let it burn safely. You have created a circle of light and therefore you need to sit comfortably in the center of this circle.

After having completed the setup of your room, you are now ready to begin your meditation. Close your eyes and focus on your breathing. Take deep breaths slowly, until you feel completely relaxed. Breathe slowly, effortlessly. Focus on the area surrounding your body, becoming aware of your weight. Picture that you are sitting on top of the earth, connecting to its energy in its entirety. The earth is supporting and protecting you throughout this session. The black gemstones have great protective powers and they will join forces, so that you remain safe and secure in this ritual.

Imagine the earth's energy springing from its depths and flooding you with light. This light is cleansing your aura, as it shines through you and removes any negative energy. Through its powerful energy, this light dissolves any negative entities that have been undermining your safety. You can sigh with relief, as you are protected by the archaic energy field of the earth. Gradually, a bubble is created around you. This is your protective shield. No ill wishes, no attachments, no malevolent gazes can get to you, as you are armored with this impenetrable bubble.

This bubble has sprung from within you, filling with the pure white light emerging from the depths of the earth. After a while, the bubble expands and reaches the walls of your room. It has become larger, so that it removes any negative energies. As you are cleansing the space around you with the bubble that is filled with bright purifying light, concentrate on the points of entry within your home. The windows and doors are enhanced, in order to provide an extra feeling of security.

Having completed the protection of your home up to this point, it is now time for the bubble to expand one last time. It becomes bigger and bigger, until it covers your whole home. Let it fill with bright light from the energy of the earth, so as to cleanse everything around you. You are completely protected by the divine nature of the earth. When you have secured everything, you can start focusing on your breathing again. Slowly breathe in and out, inhale through the nose and exhale through the mouth. Open your eyes and resume consciousness.

This meditation enables you to reinforce the protection of your home and by repeating often you can enhance its effectiveness. Do that and enjoy the safety of your dearest place on earth.

Meditation for Clear Negative Energy within Your Home

Your home is your shelter and you need to feel good when you are in it. This is non-negotiable. Unfortunately, there are times when these feelings of security, positive thinking and happiness are disrupted by stagnant energies and malevolent entities. It is therefore imperative that you perform targeted rituals to clear negative energy and purify your home.

Seat comfortably in your room, close your eyes and get into a receptive state. Connect to the energy of your home, in order to request that you change it and remove any negativity. Breathe deeply, as you are connecting to the surrounding energies. There is a lot of residual energy within your home, as it has been piling up for a long time. Request your spiritual guide or the angels that have been looking out for you to help cleanse the negative energy. Start with the room, where you spend most of your time. Visualize the conflict of the energy that has been stuck in this room.

As that energy has been built up over time, it has solidified. So by getting in the room, you get adapted to that particular energy. This can be destructive for your higher purpose. Choose to clear the atmosphere and dissolve the negativity from every corner. Do not forget to breathe deeply, releasing the tension throughout this energy cleaning session. Ask that any negativity is removed from your home. it is equally important to clear the energy from every single item of your home. Visualize that the bad vibes from through these items, leaving your home for good. Let the negative energy escape your room, go through the kitchen, up the staircases and eventually leave the house from an entry point. This is a cathartic procedure, so give this time.

When you are done, open your eyes and take some moments to relax and regain your consciousness. You will be amazed at the results you see at home. No more oppressed, heavy atmosphere. Instead, you will be glad to enter a safe haven, filled with lightness and positive vibes.

Aura Cleansing Meditation

By using the violet flame, this guided meditation is meant to help you cleanse your aura deeply. Restore your electromagnetic vibrational balance, lifting your spirit and clearing out any negative energies that conflict with your positive presence.

Close your eyes. Take a deep breath, and notice how you calm down more with each breath. Feel relaxed, as you let go of the tension. Breathe in through your nose, exhaling gently from the mouth. Visualize a violet light coming down from the sky on the top of your head. This bright light sits on your Crown chakra. Observe the light and every detail. Feel the energy, as it runs through your body. Imagine yourself bathed in that precious, divine light. Visualize your face, as you are smiling blissfully.

The powerful light melts away any negative entities, any stagnant energies within your body. This violet light transforms any negativity, absorbing it completely. Call upon your guardian angels and protectors to help you become more serene, dissolving negative spirits and maintaining your inner balance. Request that this abundant violent light shines upon your aura, sealing it against any threat. Visualize your aura getting fortified by the light.

Hold on to that feeling of knowing that you are thoroughly protected against any negative energy or malevolence trying to harm you. This is a precious feeling of utter joy and satisfaction. The violet light that has come from above offered you this feeling generously. Experience happiness and don't let go of that feeling. Instead, expand it all around your body.

Meditate in silence, as you are contemplating this wonderful experience of protection and aura cleansing. You have been blessed with the purification of your aura and you feel wonderful about it. Breathe in and out slowly, gently, effortlessly. Be present in the moment, without any distractions or obstacles getting in the way. You are happy, utterly and completely joyful.

When you feel good about yourself, open your eyes and slowly regain consciousness. Continue breathing deeply, remembering how wonderful that experience was. You feel lighter than ever before. More than that, you feel illuminated. Stretch your body and feel the calmness all around you. You are revived, filled with energy and pleasure.

Remember to repeat the same ritual every time you feel like you lack energy and liveliness. Since your aura is not static, it fluctuates in size and so you need to make sure that you take care of it.

Meditation with the Angels for Clearing Negative Energy

The angels can be of paramount assistance to you, in your endeavor to release any negativity from your body or your surroundings. It is important that you maintain your calmness throughout this guided meditation. Release any bad vibe, allowing yourself to sigh with relief at the thought of having dissolved negative energies all around.

Close your eyes, breathe in and out gently and feel your body relax with every breath. Focus on your intentions and firmly request assistance from your guardian angels: *"Archangel Michael, archangel Raphael, I seek your presence here. I want you to come and support me in my effort to remove negative energies and restore goodness."* Suddenly, you will start feeling their presence nearby. They will come to help you, protecting you against all harm.

Relax even further and visualize a pure white light. The light shines bright all the way from the sky to your crown, on top of your head. It enters your body through the Crown chakra and runs smoothly through all the energy centers until your feet. The light flows through you and reaches your aura, cleansing it and filling it with positive high vibrational frequencies. Eventually, the light passes through you and connects to the very center of the earth. This is the divine energy in perfect alignment.

Since this divine pure light has shone through you, you need to draw your attention to your inner self. You will see a light shining brighter than ever before from within you. This light is connected to your life force, becoming stronger every single moment. The archangels are standing very close to you. They protect you during this process. So feel this inner power of yours glowing and expanding. Repeat positive affirmations about your enlightenment: *"I am a powerful human being, filled with divine light."*

You are in charge of the energies that flow through you. It is in your power to choose which energies to allow and which ones to reject. No one else has that power over you. This is something you need to believe in, as you are visualizing your omnipotence.

Now archangel Raphael comes closer, healing you and your energy. You feel the comfort from this experience, repeating the following: *"I reject any negative connection that does not serve my higher purpose in life. I command that any negative energies leave my body, never to return again. I stand only in the light and love of my Creator."*

Open your eyes, breathe in and out slowly and take a few

moments to resume your consciousness. This is an intense meditation, which requires the divine protection of the archangels. After that, you will feel more confident, loving of yourself and independent.

Guided Meditation to Heal Past Trauma

Past lives can affect you in many ways. If you have been stuck in a problematic situation, unable to move forward, then it is essential that you revisit your past lives and figure out how to push through. Sometimes you need to heal a traumatic experience from another life, before being able to move forward with your current one.

Close your eyes and think of a place where you seem to come back to again and again. This can be a loop from a different lifetime, representing an experience that has made you stuck. Breathe in through your nose and out through your mouth. Relax and let go of your concerns, your thoughts, your traumas. Feel the energy into your soul get in your physical body, as you are exhaling gently. This process makes you feel grounded, aware of the slightest part of your body.

Even though you will remain in your physical body, your thoughts will wander along with your soul. Through your mind, you will have the chance to envision everything absolutely clearly, under the guidance and constant protection of your angels. You will gradually feel your body getting heavier. Now, focus on your third eye. Breathe deeply, as you are feeling your Crown and Third Eye chakras open up. Drift into the past. Be open-minded to what you are about to discover.

You will notice energies that are floating. Request that they show you where you have been stuck, so that you can release yourself from this ongoing ordeal. You need to move forward in your current lifetime. As you delve deeper, you will see images of your past lives run before your eyes. Embrace them without judgment. This is a very delicate procedure, until you manage to envision the experience that has caused your trauma.

As soon as you discover this traumatic experience, you need to gather details about it by settling more comfortably. What year is it? In which country are you located? What language are you speaking? Take a look around you and observe every little detail. Remind yourself that you are just an observer and therefore you don't have to be afraid.

Watch your trauma as it unfolds, knowing that you are safe at all times. Process what has happened, breathing deeply and remaining calm throughout the entire experience. After having observed everything clearly, you need to express your gratitude. Say *"thank you"* for the important lesson that this experience has given to you. Acknowledge that it had to happen, so that you could evolve in your next lives. Forgive, love and remember. Release negative energy with every exhale.

Now it is time to get back to your physical body. Feel the protective presence of the archangels, holding your hand throughout your travel and until you have settled to your physical presence. Inhale and exhale deeply, feeling your spirit extremely lighter than before. Bring your thoughts to the present moment, revaluating the situation that had been causing you discomfort.

22

CHAPTER 11: THE 7 DAY NEGATIVE ENERGY CLEANSE RITUAL TO ENCHANT YOUR HOME WITH ANGELIC POWER

What does it take for you to call on your guardian angels for help? How can you request their presence and seek their unconditional support in your endeavors? It is true that angels are always by your side, even if you cannot see them. More often than not, we get to feel their presence around us. We are sure that they are right by our side every step of the way, no matter how long it takes for us to stop needing them.

Our connection with the angels is profoundly spiritual. It enables us to communicate with the divine and feel safe in a world filled with dangers lurking in every corner. It is a dangerous place we live in, but our spiritual guides are always here to lay a helping hand and offer their wisdom. This is how we pull through, get it together and survive any hardships that emerge along the way.

After having analyzed several different aspects of clearing the energy within your home and your body, the only thing that's missing is a practical approach for your everyday life. I know that I have promised you in the title that you can get tangible results for spiritual cleansing in just 7 days. In fact, you will see that a week is more than enough, if you follow my guidelines below.

The daily ritual secret formula that I have designed for you is able to reset the energy within your home. You will not need to spend your entire day trying different time-consuming rituals for removing all bad vibes from your personal sanctuary. On the contrary, these steps that I have included within the formula are easy to implement in your daily routine. They are also fun and you will most likely end up sticking with these morning habits, even after the completion of your experimental week.

Be open-minded about this week. Wake up with an optimistic feeling, a sensation that everything is going to be alright. In this way, you are going to attract these positive vibes and cast away any negative thoughts trying to creep into your mind. The Law of Attraction works and therefore you should follow its principles to skyrocket your potential in life. You must keep the faith, as this is a helpful asset in your attempt to improve your life on so many different levels.

Even if you get bored or lack the will to perform your morning ritual, you are advised not to slip up. You need to be consistent, so as to provide optimum results in the end. If you sleep in and wake up later than usual, make the necessary adjustments, in order to fit this ritual into your busy schedule. Do not postpone or delay or cancel your energy cleansing. If you do, you will soon realize that negative entities are far more persistent—After all, perseverance is often the key to success.

Negative Energy Cleansing Daily Ritual Secret Formula

As you are reaching the end of this book, it is essential that you have all the tools you are going to need towards clearing negative energy and malevolent spirits from your home. Below, you can see a secret formula you can use as a daily ritual. This will help you purify your home in as little as

7 days. Be consistent and detailed when performing this ritual. It consists of simple things that you can easily do on a daily basis. The ritual is fast, requiring no more than 30 minutes of your time. Wake up in the morning, open the windows to let the fresh air in and allow the sun to flood the room. Wear your widest smile and start your day with the following secret formula.

Step 1: Express Your Gratitude

Start your day every morning, by expressing what you are grateful for in your life. Is it your family, a newborn kid that has added to your happiness, or maybe your career? Be extremely detailed when you are saying *"thank you"* for specific things in life you have received. Rather than say *"thank you for my work,"* you can just as easily say *"thank you for the wonderful opportunity I have been given at work to collaborate with one of the best associates in the company."* The former statement is too generic, whereas the latter fills you with a higher vibrational frequency right away.

This step should take around 5 minutes. You can keep a journal if you want. Otherwise, simply close your eyes and meditate. Express your gratitude out loud, channeling it to the things that bring you joy and make you feel satisfied. As soon as you start doing that, you will instantly feel better. You will realize how much you already have, which is always a great reminder in case you have taken that for granted. Being conscious of what you have accomplished is amazing, as it boosts your self-confidence and makes you feel good about yourself.

Step 2: Practice EFT Tapping

You are now ready to move forward to the next step and raise your vibration. One of the coolest ways to do so is by practicing EFT tapping. Concentrate on your head and the area of the neck, the chest and armpits for this quick, yet effective tapping session. It doesn't have to be anything elaborate. You just begin tapping the external part of your palm, as you are repeating positive affirmations about yourself. You can say that you are awesome, you are a great worker, you are devoted to your goals or you are an extrovert. Whatever makes your heart beat faster, you should express it through these affirmations.

By tapping on the forehead, your third eye right between your eyebrows, the area under your eyes and your cheekbones, your upper lip and chin, you can continue repeating those amazing affirmations. They will make you feel much better, by elevating your vibrational frequencies even further. Tapping creates vibrations that are beneficial to your well-being. When combined with verbal stimulants that promote joy and satisfaction, the result is even more impressive. Typically, an EFT tapping session will take you about 10 minutes.

Step 3: Use Essential Oils

What a better way to start your day than with the intoxicating fragrances of essential oils! I have referred earlier in this book to the powerful healing properties of lemongrass. However, you can try out different essential oils that clear negative energy and boost your mood. Just use an essential oil diffuser to spread the aromas all over the place. In fact, you can combine that with drinking a warm cup of herbal tea or chamomile. This will give you the chance to hydrate, soothe your soul and wake up naturally.

Some of the best essential oils to use besides lemongrass include peppermint, sweet orange, rosemary, cypress and juniper berry. Along with the use of essential oils, you can also burn Palo Santo wood. It smells amazing, cleansing the atmosphere from any negative energies piling up in the room. If you have the items at hand, this step will require 10 minutes of your time along with the preparation of your liquid bliss to sip on.

Step 4: Visualizations

You have already heightened your vibrational frequencies, so you must be feeling over the moon. In order to make the most of your morning ritual, you should not forget to include visualizations in the mix. These visualizations will offer you the opportunity to manifest exactly what you want to attract in your life, so that they are drawn by your energy. This is a lovely way to increase your vibration, while at the same time experiencing your desires right now. Instead of projecting your desire into the future, you live as if you have already acquired what you are looking for.

By visualizing that you are accomplished, happy, abundant and successful, healthy and outgoing, you experience the emotions flowing through these states. How would you feel if you were successful in your profession? Try to visualize that and see what it means for you, emotionally-wise. Again, this step usually requires 5 minutes to complete.

Step 5: Tidy Your Room

I am sure you are well aware of the significance of a tidied place by now. After completing these 4 steps that have filled you with joy and have skyrocketed your energy from within, it is important to tidy up your room a little. Of course, I am not talking about dusting or vacuuming. These chores can be parts of a deeper cleaning that takes place once a week or so. I am referring to the powerful effects of making your bed and cleaning your workspace, your armchair, your bedside table and anything else you keep within reach.

By doing so, you remain grounded and you feel accomplished about having done something meaningful so early on in your day. Making your bed is an excellent way to remain disciplined, organized and in line with your inner balance. No more than 5 minutes will be enough, assuming that you keep everything in place.

Step 5+1: Use Your DIY Spray

To wrap things up with your morning ritual, take a

moment and use your powerful DIY spray to remove negative energy. This spray contains rose petals, which are extremely high in vibrational frequencies. It also contains sage, which is a potent purifier and cleanser of energy. Along with water, these wonderful ingredients create a secret formula that works wonders for your personal space.

Just spray the cleansing spray and rinse. This can be used daily and you can even spray it on yourself, as it contains no chemicals or preservatives. It is 100% natural and organic, offering a great option for cleaning and removing any negativity. Once more, you will need 5 minutes to complete this step.

Tips for the Best Daily Ritual

You should adhere to the morning ritual I have laid out for you for at least 7 days. During this time, you will certainly notice a remarkable change in the energy of your home. In fact, the negative energies will disappear and in their place you will feel the lightness of positivity. Your sleep will improve and you will have no issues bothering you for no actual reason.

After a week has passed, you are free to continue with this ritual on a daily basis. If you do, you will see that things are only getting better. Incorporate some of the guided meditations I have created for you and you will never have to deal with such negative energies again in your life.

If you want to enhance the power of your visualizations, you can also use crystals and gemstones. Black obsidian, onyx and black tourmaline are exquisite for clearing the negative energy, as you know. A wide range of precious stones and crystals can be found in the market, ready to help you reach your goals much faster. In addition, you can experiment with several other healing items. Scented candles, Tibetan singing bowls, amulets and talismans, are all going to boost your own powers and take you higher.

A Nighttime Ritual to Cleanse Your Energy

You have spent an entire day on the go, performing your scheduled tasks and mingling with a lot of people. Now the time has come for you to return home, in the comfort of your personal shelter. You are in your safe haven and you want nothing more than to relax, letting go of the tension and enjoying precious moments alone, or with those you hold dear to you.

First of all, it is good that you take a soothing shower before going to bed. I am guessing not many people can indulge in a bath with salts and essential oils every single night. However, you can have a warm shower and use products that help you relax. Let the water run through your skin and remove any toxic thought, along with dead skin cells and dust. Let go of the evil eye, as well as any other negative energy that has been accumulated on your body.

As soon as you finish showering, you should rinse your skin with a soft towel and begin your beauty routine. Do whatever makes you happy; use a scrub to exfoliate your skin, apply moisturizing cream to hydrate your body and comb your hair. When you get into the bedroom, make sure that you have created a welcoming, relaxing atmosphere. Play some soothing, inspirational music in the background. You can use mantras, if you want. Otherwise, any relaxing music will do.

Light a candle or two. Dim the lights or use the candlelight as your sole source of brightness within the room. Burn incense with your favorite fragrances. I would suggest using camphor, as it allows you to clear the negative energy and rejuvenate. Concentrate on your breathing and meditate for a few moments. Close your eyes, listening to the sounds of the mantras or relaxing music in the distance. Picture a bright light on the crown of your head, slowly moving downwards and filling you with its overwhelming power.

Experience this moment of pure bright light filling you from within, flooding every organ, every part of your body, every cell. Visualize the light expanding and reaching your aura. Feel your aura as it gets purified, utterly cleansed by the divine light. This visualization helps you align your energy centers, creating a connection between the grounded energy of the earth and the mystical energy of the divine. With that in mind, keep breathing deeply and concentrate on the present.

Finish your visualization with a wide smile on your face. Avoid any artificial light and steer clear from any electronic device for at least an hour before bedtime. Once you lie down, close your eyes and manifest your desires. Have those positive thoughts in your mind, as you are drifting away in the sweetest dreams. You will be enjoying a restful night, having cleared the negative energies within your room and having balanced your inner energy. Good night!

23
AFTERWORD

You have successfully reached the final chapter of my book. I hope that you have found it helpful, in your attempt to interpret the spiritual world and delve into the mysteries of the divine. It is amazing what you can do in your life, simply by aligning your energy with the energy of the cosmos. By now you have discovered what it feels like to be cursed or the victim of the evil eye and you have learned how to cleanse your aura and energy chakras.

Furthermore, you have read through guided meditations that allow you to practice what you have been taught theoretically about negative energies, unwanted guests and entities from a different world. This has been a wonderful journey in the mystical philosophies of the world, dictating that you need to find the balance from within yourself, before you are able to thrive in your life. First, you have to cleanse your own body and soul, before you move on to the next level and purify your direct environment.

There are evil entities out there, wanting to do you harm. However, this should not bring you down or lead you to despair. Besides, you are not alone in this world. You have a network of family members, friends and of course your spiritual guides to help you out in times of need. This book has hopefully inspired you to further elaborate on spirituality and the mysteries lying beneath the surface. It would be great if you followed up with more information about several other parts of the divine world.

Introduce healthy practices in your life, such as performing meditations, yoga and Pilates, EFT tapping, TRE and Reiki. All these techniques aim at boosting your vibration to make you healthier and happier in your life. Isn't this what you have been searching for? If you could accomplish that in an all-natural, non-invasive manner, then it would make no sense to reject such an offer. There are methods that have been conceived out of pure necessity. These methods have been proven extremely useful when dealing with the spiritual world.

Another piece of advice from me would be to join communities of like-minded people. In this way, you will be able to discuss the things that matter to you the most. They will understand you, offering their own wisdom and practical information that might end up saving your life. You should not be afraid to express your needs and desires. Find the right people to surround you, so as to feel comfortable talking about what is troubling you. Communication is a key element in forming healthy relationships, after all.

Looking back at the time when I wrote *"Spiritual Cleans-*

ing: Soul Cleansing Secrets No One Talks About & How To Cleanse Negative Energy From Your House In 7 Days (Positive Energy For Home)," I feel grateful and happy. It is my honor to be able and share my hard-earned knowledge on the subject. Through my experiments with different approaches, I have read thousands of books and I have spoken to thousands of people. What I have obtained from every single one of them is literally invaluable.

Now that you have read through my book, I hope that we meet again soon. I am wishing you love, light and courage on your journey. By taking initiative and getting all the way through this book, you have completed the most difficult part of the entire process. This was a fantastic idea and you have so many wonderful things to look forward to now that you have read all about it!

REFERENCES

andreas160578. (2016a). *Salt Spa Wellness.* https://pixabay.com/photos/salt-spa-wellness-wood-1884166/

Anthony, K. (2017, December). *EFT Tapping.* Healthline; Healthline Media. https://www.healthline.com/health/eft-tapping

Bejan, A., & Lorente, S. (2010). The constructal law of design and evolution in nature. *Philosophical Transactions of the Royal Society B: Biological Sciences, 365*(1545), 1335–1347. https://doi.org/10.1098/rstb.2009.0302

Bledsoe, D. A. (2013, October 1). *The Evil Eye: Ancient, Yet Contemporary Phenomenon and a Biblical Response.* Missionexus.org. https://missionexus.org/the-evil-eye-ancient-yet-contemporary-phenomenon-and-a-biblical-response/

Camille Noe Pagán. (2018, January 11). *What Is Aromatherapy?* WebMD; WebMD. https://www.webmd.com/balance/stress-management/aromatherapy-overview#1

Collins, N. (2016, July 14). *Science Says Burning Sage Can Clean The Air And Improve Your Health.* Lifehack. https://www.lifehack.org/426156/science-says-burning-sage-can-clean-the-air-and-improve-your-health

REFERENCES

Corbin, K. (n.d.). *The Law of Attraction and Quantum Physics – Law of Attraction Resource Guide*. Https://Www.Lawofattractionresourceguide.com/. https://www.lawofattractionresourceguide.com/the-law-of-attraction-and-quantum-physics/

dhandapani, basker. (2017). Angel Woman White. https://pixabay.com/photos/angel-woman-white-girl-young-2816236/

Fiona, K. (2017). *Buddha Relax Relaxation*. https://pixabay.com/photos/buddha-relax-relaxation-asia-2109894/

freeAgent42, T. K. @. (2018, October 22). *"The field is the sole governing agency of the particle" Einstein*. Medium. https://medium.com/@tonyknight_92437/the-field-is-the-sole-governing-agency-of-the-particle-einstein-1f770090a926

Glady. (2013). *Rose Flower Dew*. https://pixabay.com/photos/rose-flower-dew-dewdrops-droplets-165819/

hassan, mohamed. (2018). *Meditation Zen Chan*. https://pixabay.com/photos/meditation-zen-chan-yoga-statue-3338691/

ImagesBG. (2017a). *Meditation Nature Yoga*. https://pixabay.com/photos/meditation-nature-yoga-sun-clouds-2001317/

Lolame. (2018). *Candles Still Life*. https://pixabay.com/photos/candles-still-life-candlestick-3493575/

M, R. (2019). An Overview of the Thymus. EndocrineWeb. https://www.endocrineweb.com/endocrinology/overview-thymus

Mannonen, T. (2016). Crystals Stones Healing Mystic. https://pixabay.com/photos/crystals-stones-healing-mystic-1567953/

Markus1308. (2020). *Bank Nature Bench*. https://pixabay.com/photos/bank-nature-bench-rest-loneliness-5103277/

McCutcheon, S. (2018). Positive Thinking Energy. https://pixabay.com/photos/positive-thinking-energy-reiki-3805169/

monicore. (2016b). Essential Oils Aromatherapy.

REFERENCES

https://pixabay.com/photos/essential-oils-aromatherapy-spa-oil-1433694/

Pexels. (2016c). *Alternative Energy Aura.* https://pixabay.com/photos/alternative-energy-aura-energetic-1869248/

Pexels. (2016). Meditate Meditation Peaceful. https://pixabay.com/photos/meditate-meditation-peaceful-1851165/

Photo, D. (2017). Self Confidence Force Woman. https://pixabay.com/photos/self-confidence-force-wave-sea-2036236/

Photos, F. (2015). *Sunset Dusk Silhouette.* https://pixabay.com/photos/sunset-dusk-silhouette-shadow-girl-691848/

Pitkanen, M. (2018, June). *(PDF) The experiments of Masaru Emoto with emotional imprinting of water.* ResearchGate. https://www.researchgate.net/publication/335909571_The_experiments_of_Masaru_Emoto_with_emotional_imprinting_of_water

piro4d. (2016b). *Feng Shui Zen Stones.* https://pixabay.com/photos/feng-shui-zen-stones-texture-1927590/

sorcel. (2014). Amulet Evil Eyes. https://pixabay.com/photos/amulet-evil-eyes-turkey-blue-charm-458235/

StockSnap. (2017). *People Woman Happy.* https://pixabay.com/photos/people-woman-happy-relax-travel-2588546/

vetsikas1969, dimitris. (2020). *Girl Meditation Nature.* https://pixabay.com/photos/girl-meditation-nature-yoga-4981766/

Voicu, A. (2016). Woman Beauty Wreath. https://pixabay.com/photos/woman-beauty-wreath-fashion-1403458/

Wikipedia Contributors. (2019, May 8). Atlas (mythology). Wikipedia; Wikimedia Foundation. https://en.wikipedia.org/wiki/Atlas_(mythology)

PLEASE LEAVE A REVIEW ON AMAZON

From the bottom of my heart, thank you for reading my book. I truly hope that it helps you on your spiritual journey and to live a more empowered and happy life. Would you be kind enough to leave an honest review for this book on Amazon? I would be ecstatic to read your feedback and it could impact the lives of others across the globe, giving them hope and power. I read **every** review I receive and each one helps me become the best writer I can be.

Thank you and good luck,

Angela Grace

JOIN OUR COMMUNITY

Why not join our Facebook community and discuss your spiritual path with like-minded seekers?

We would love to hear from you!

Go here to join the Ascending Vibrations community: ***bit.ly/ascendingvibrations***

CLAIM YOUR FREE AUDIOBOOK

DOWNLOAD THE *'SPIRITUAL CLEANSING'* AUDIOBOOK INSTANTLY FOR FREE

If you love listening to audio books on-the-go, I have great news for you. You can download the audiobook version of *'Spiritual Cleansing'* for **FREE** just by signing up for a **FREE** 30-day audible trial! Turn the page for more details!

CLAIM YOUR FREE AUDIOBOOK

Audible trial benefits

As an audible customer, you'll receive the below benefits with you 30-day free trial:

• Free audible copy of this book
• After the trial, you will get 1 credit each month to use on any audiobook
• Your credits automatically roll over to the next month if you don't use them
• Choose from over 400,000 titles
• Listen anywhere with the audible app across multiple devices
• Make easy, no hassle exchanges of any audiobook you don't love
• Keep your audiobooks forever, even if you cancel your membership
• And much more

Click the links below to get started:

Go here for audible US:
bit.ly/spiritualcleansinglisten
Go here for audible UK:
bit.ly/spiritualcleansinglistenuk

www.ingramcontent.com/pod-product-compliance
Lightning Source LLC
Chambersburg PA
CBHW021441070526
44577CB00002B/236